0·4474

88
OC

D1612966

THE DRUG-LIKE
BRONTË DREAM

THE DRUG-LIKE BRONTË DREAM

MARGARET LANE

Illustrated by

JOAN HASSALL

JOHN MURRAY · LONDON

© Margaret Lane 1952, 1968, 1979, 1980

First published 1980
by John Murray (Publishers) Ltd
50 Albemarle Street, London WIX 4BD

All rights reserved
Unauthorised duplication
contravenes applicable laws

Printed in Great Britain by
Latimer Trend & Company Ltd, Plymouth

British Library Cataloguing in Publication Data

Lane, Margaret, *b.* 1907
The drug-like Brontë dream.
1. Brontë family
2. English fiction   19th century   History
and criticism
I. Title
823'.8'09   PR4169
ISBN 0-7195-3768-1

Dedicated
with affection
to Donald Hopewell

Acknowledgment

OF THE four essays in *The Drug-like Brontë Dream*, three were originally given as addresses in Haworth to the Brontë Society, and one at the Cheltenham Festival of Literature. I mention this because it was due to the kind encouragement of the Brontë Society that they have now taken modest shape as a book. I would also like to thank them for allowing me to use Mrs Gaskell's haunting sketch of Haworth (which is in their archives) for the book jacket and endpapers.

Miss Joan Hassall, who engraved the original illustrations for my earlier biographical study, *The Brontë Story*, has kindly given permission for some of them to be used in the present volume, in addition to her other engravings that are printed for the first time. Mr Richard Harrison, who now owns the originals, was generous in lending them. I am grateful to them both.

M.L.

Contents

Introduction

Introduction

IT IS NOT EASY, arriving in Haworth today by smoothly graded roads sweeping into a capacious car-park, to recognise the gaunt and stony village of our imagination. Even the precipitous cobbled street, basically unchangeable, is wearing a pantomime disguise, decked out in pottery, craft-ware, souvenirs, postcards. And in summer a constant stream of bemused strangers, staring in the repetitive shop-windows, licking their ice-creams.

Yet the spell persists. In winter, even in late autumn, when the crowds have gone, a thousand details become not only visible but recognisable. The tidy hedges round the Parsonage fade and vanish, leaving the garden plot open to that leaden sea of gravestones in the churchyard. The house itself shrinks to its old dimensions, loses that strangely incongruous ornament (a metal sign dangling above a tea-shop?) and moves back into the past. A sense of illusion comes and goes; there are moments of awareness when we are back in the Haworth that Mrs Gaskell sketched with such eerie vision in 1855, after Charlotte's death, capturing for ever the little naked Parsonage, diminished church, staggering gravestones, bleak open moor and background of bare hills.

'Dingy and commonplace' was how Virginia Woolf described Haworth when she saw it in 1904. 'There is nothing remarkable about a mid-Victorian parsonage, though tenanted by genius.' True, in a sense; and in another sense not true. The power of strange imaginative genius, in both Charlotte and Emily Brontë, makes it difficult for us, even today, to look at that industrialised and sooty landscape without emotion.

The temptation, too, to examine and interpret is as strong as ever. Fortunately, both Charlotte and Mrs Gaskell were communicative by nature. Their letters can almost be read as autobiographies; their recipients had the wit to realise this, and so preserve them. As time has passed we have learned more and more about Charlotte's creative beginnings, her inner nature, personality, unique experience. But about her sisters Emily and Anne and their brother Branwell we are almost as much in the dark as we ever were, and the unending spate of doctoral theses, I fear, is unlikely to enlighten us.

All that we continue to absorb and deduce about this remarkable family tells us that they were a rare species, distinctly Celtic in origin and flavour, a surprising crop to have been sown by an obscure and penniless Irish curate. (But Patrick Brontë, as we know, was himself something of an intellectual phenomenon.) It is ironic that in the early years the greatest hopes and expectations were of Branwell, only boy in a family of five girls; but this is part of a traditional domestic pattern. A facile brilliance, the gift of being good company among cronies, a belief in one's own talents are not enough. Nothing of Branwell's that survives has the smallest spark of life, and the gradual realisation of his own ineptitude undoubtedly played its part in the decline, through brandy and laudanum, into a sorry death. Yet his presence is still perceptible in the work of his three surviving sisters. With Charlotte, his story-telling partnership through childhood and adolescence set her on an obsessive course from which she later withdrew, recognising hidden danger. Anne, the sister who had the most intimate knowledge of Branwell's weakness, since for three years they worked together in the same alien environment as governess and tutor, distilled her disillusioning experience in *The Tenant of Wildfell Hall*, a story of the rapid decay of a charming profligate and drunkard.

Of Branwell's influence on Emily I suppose we shall never hear the end. I find myself sceptical of the endless theories that echo from academic circles in different parts of the world. Emily Brontë remains an enigma; wholly secretive regarding herself, self-contained, personally uncommunicative. Even in her most haunting poems she speaks from a hidden place, like a veiled sibyl.

The latest hypothesis that I have come across sees Branwell as the inspiration of Heathcliff, and drug-addiction as the cause and explanation of everything strange, brutal and demented about that dominating anti-hero. The argument is ingenious, but leaves me unconvinced. It is rarely safe to discriminate between experience and imagination in the work of a great writer; in the case of Emily Brontë it is impossible. 'All true histories,' wrote her sister Anne, 'contain instruction; though, in some, the treasure may be hard to find, and, when found, so trivial in quantity, that the dry, shrivelled kernel scarcely compensates for the trouble of cracking the nut.'

In the following four essays, three of which were delivered as addresses to the Brontë Society and one at the Cheltenham Festival of Literature, I have not attempted the cracking of any hard nuts. Instead, I have tried to clarify my own conclusions on several aspects of Brontë

history: the magical beginnings, in which all four
children formed productive and hallucinated partnerships;
the dominant influence, particularly in Charlotte's life, of
the private schoolroom; the still unfathomable enigma of
Emily Brontë; and the thousand-to-one chance that
brought Mrs Gaskell on to the late and lonely scene as a
benign influence in Charlotte's life and, in the end, her
incomparable biographer.

1980   *Margaret Lane*

I

'The Drug-like Brontë Dream . . .'

I

'The Drug-like Brontë Dream . . .'

THAT PHRASE, when first I came upon it, acted for me like the sudden switching-on of a searchlight, a beam revealing an unexpected path which has been fascinating to follow.

Anyone who has read Miss Fanny Ratchford's two books, *Legends of Angria* and *The Brontës' Web of Childhood*, will know that they contain the most painstaking examination of those minute writings which the Brontës produced throughout childhood and youth, and of which there are many examples now safely housed in the Parsonage Museum. The history of those tiny manuscripts is interesting. After Charlotte Brontë's death, those that survived—all of them Charlotte's and Branwell's and none, alas, of Emily's or Anne's—passed into Mr Nicholls's possession, and went with him when he finally left Haworth and removed to Ireland. There they lay undisturbed until 1894, when Mr Clement Shorter, the literary journalist, went to Ireland at the instigation of Mr T. J. Wise (book collector, and, as we now know, literary forger) to buy up any available Brontëana. Mr Nicholls sold all the letters in his possession and the juvenile manuscripts, which had lain wrapped in newspapers at the bottom of a cupboard for more than thirty years, 'where,' as he afterwards wrote to Mr Shorter, 'had it not been for your visit, they must have remained during my life-time, and most likely afterwards been destroyed'.

The little manuscripts were broken up by Mr Wise, who selected a few specimens for his own library, and following his usual practice as literary speculator, gradually introduced the rest into the sale-room. They were eagerly bought by collectors and soon became widely scattered through Europe and America. Fortunately a good number came finally into the hands of Mr Henry Bonnell of Philadelphia, who bequeathed them to the Brontë Museum. A number found their way to the library of Texas University, where Miss Ratchford began her long work of deciphering and studying them, together with any other specimens which were accessible, until she realised that they were not simply the curious scraps that Mrs Gaskell and everyone else had thought them, but, as she revealed, 'a closely connected series of stories, poems, novels, histories and dramas, having a common setting and common characters, written through the sixteen years between 1829 and 1845, a period comprehending approximately one-third of Charlotte's life'.

Now, it is not extraordinary that a group of gifted children should evolve an elaborate play-world, with sustained characters, to which they remain devoted for a number of years. I dare say we have all of us, at our various levels, done something of the kind in childhood, and can remember impersonating our favourite characters for days on end. What was extraordinary about the Brontës' games was that they produced an extensive and precocious literature, and, as the children grew up, provided a fantasy world which for all of them, at various times, became a substitute for life.

It is at this point that Miss Ratchford's phrase 'the drug-like Brontë dream' lights up the path. Briefly the

conclusion to which that path has brought me is this—
that all four of them, Charlotte, Branwell, Emily and
Anne, were involved in a profound turning away from, or
refusal of, ordinary life; that they spun their separate, and
quite different substitutes for it, out of their own
imaginations, and that they became addicted to their day-
dream world as completely as an addict to his drug.

There is nothing new, to the psychologist, in this idea
of rejecting real life, with all its harshness and its problems,
and substituting for it some more acceptable fantasy.
Most of us, unless we are particularly happy and fortunate, do it in some degree; and all of us can call to mind
people whose day-dreams about themselves and their lives
are very different indeed from the reality. Freud himself
long ago stated the matter with great insight and sympathy. 'Life as we find it,' he wrote, 'is too hard for us: it
entails too much pain; too many disappointments;
impossible tasks. We cannot do without palliative reme-
dies . . . powerful diversions of interest, which lead us to
care little about our misery; substitutive gratifications,
which lessen it; and intoxicating substances, which make
us insensitive to it. Something of the kind is indispens-
able.' Now day-dreams, which on the Brontë level of
intensity are nothing if not a 'powerful diversion of
interest,' have been made suspect in our time by psycho-
analysis, and they certainly can conceal great dangers;
but they are also the forcing-ground of the imagination.
Bertrand Russell once wisely said that they are an
essential part of the creative mind; the danger is that
'when throughout a long life there is no means of relating
them to reality they easily become unwholesome and even
dangerous to sanity'. This is, to a marked degree, what

happened to Branwell; and Emily Brontë is the only writer of genius we know of who completely rejected actual life and embraced, with perfect steadiness, a passionate and poetic existence lived entirely at a high level of the imagination. Some poets—Coleridge through opium, Wordsworth in his moments of mystical experience, Blake—have reached levels of intuition and expression with which ordinary life and consciousness have nothing to do; but Emily Brontë seems to have lived the whole of her creative life as poet and novelist at this level, without the aid of any drug beyond the obsessive daydream which all four children in their different ways created. Charlotte in maturity recognised the dangers of the mirage, and deliberately broke out of it. Emily stayed resolutely within it, like some self-communing votary in her cell, so achieving freedom for the development of her genius—an unselfconscious masculine freedom which in real life her difficult temperament might never have allowed. Branwell dwelt in the drug-like dream too long, taking refuge from his fears and secret inadequacies. Anne's sad refuge was in that twilight of religious melancholy which is to me the most tragic part of her short history. On all of them its influence was profound.

The special quality of the Brontë genius, as manifested in both Charlotte and Emily, was in essence the same—another point that Miss Ratchford's perception has made clear. 'It has become the fashion,' she says 'to exalt Emily and debase Charlotte, in utter ignorance that their genius—the ability to realise the imaginative with the vivid intensity of the actual — was identical, and that Emily's one point of superiority was her full surrender to the creative spirit which Charlotte fought with all the strength of her tyrannical conscience.' It was this very quality of their genius which enabled both of them to develop the drug-like dream into such a powerful obsession. In Charlotte's case it had elements of real danger, because of the conflict between the day-dream and reality—a conflict which brought her at times to the verge of mental breakdown.

We all know the beginning of the story—how Mr Brontë brought home the box of wooden soldiers when the children were small, and how, out of the imaginary adventures of these toys, they evolved the Young Men's Play, the Play of the Islanders, and eventually all the long sagas of Angria and Gondal. Charlotte and Branwell, being older, are at first the prime movers in all these plays. They work together; their collaboration is complete; yet even in this first period of the play-writing the little books reveal great differences between them. Charlotte's work, for all its childish extravagance, is never safe to dismiss as merely tedious; in nearly every page there is a phrase, an idea, a line of description which catches the attention; while Branwell's, written with the same enthusiasm and equally abundant, achieves a dullness which makes it unreadable. His battles, slaughterings and heavy humour weary the eye to the point where it no longer takes in the sense—which is what happens to anyone who has the stamina to follow the deadening tramp, tramp of Branwell's poetry. Charlotte's output is so prodigious that it suggests not only a most unchildlike concentration on this chosen game, but a disregard of all other possibilities of amusement. The intensity of her application can be judged from a note she made herself on a tiny volume of nearly three thousand words which she wrote when she was thirteen. 'I began this book on the 22 of February 1830 and finished it on the 23 of February 1830 doing 3 pages on the first day and 11 on the second. On the first day I wrote an hour and a half in the morning, and an hour and a half in the evening. On the second day I wrote a quarter of an hour in the morning, 2 hours in the afternoon, and a quarter of an hour in the evening, making in the whole 5 hours and a half.' Many a grown-up and established author would give much for such concentration and production.

As time goes on, and fulfils none of the promises of childhood, Charlotte takes refuge more and more continuously in her imaginary world. It becomes a secret, shared with her sisters and her brother. Outsiders, even intimate friends like Mary Taylor and Ellen Nussey, are allowed no glimpse of it. Charlotte is growing up; the awakening emotions of a singularly intense and passionate nature, having no outlet in real life, are given free expression in the exciting hot-house atmosphere of the dream. This secret world, the 'world below,' the 'infernal world' as she and Branwell called it, is nourished on Byron's poetry, on Gothic romances, on a heated imagination. It is a world where heroes are amoral and unscrupulous, 'viciously beautiful,' handsome dukes who possess noble wives and passionate mistresses, who beget bastards, ruin their friends and are at all times wonderfully sardonic and eccentric and sadistic. By the time she is twenty, unhappy and lonely as a teacher at Miss Wooler's, and taking continuous refuge in her day-dream from a life she can hardly bear, one gets the impression that the intensity of her self-induced visions has brought her to the verge of trance. The creatures of her imagination, wicked, thrilling and adored, she summons at will, as often as she dares. 'I saw them stately and handsome . . . eyes smiling, and lips moving in audible speech that I knew better than my brother's and sisters' . . . what glorious associations crowded upon me, what excitement heated my face and made me clasp my hands in ecstasy! . . . How few,' she confides to her journal, 'would believe that from sources purely imaginary such happiness could be derived! Pen cannot portray the deep interest of the scenes, of the continued train of events I have witnessed . . . What a treasure is thought! What a privilege is reverie! I am thankful I have the power of solacing myself with the dream of creations whose reality I shall never behold. May I never lose that power.'

But her pen both could and did portray these visions, in a style in which the compelling rhythms of her mature work are already audible. Listen to this: 'And then in his eye there is a shade of something, words cannot express what . . . a gleam, scarcely human, dark and fiend-like . . . Once that marvellous light fell on me; and long after I beheld it vanish, its memory haunted me like a spirit. The sensation which it excited was very singular. I felt as if he could read my soul; and strange to tell, there was no fear lest he should find sinful thoughts and recollections there, but a harrassing dread lest anything good might arise which would awaken the tremendous power of sarcasm that I saw lurking on every feature of his face.' Her heroines of this period are often absurdly extravagant, in the Gothic mode, but the speech of one at least has the note of authentic passion which later shocked the readers of *Jane Eyre*. 'The fact is, I have far keener feelings than any other human being I ever knew. I have seen a hundred times beautiful women round me, compared with whom I was in appearance only a puppet; and in mind, in imagination I knew them dull, apathetic, cold to me . . . and if Lord Douro ever thinks to be loved again with half the burning intensity with which I *have* loved him, with which I *do* love him, with which, if he were torturing me, I *should* love him, he is deluded.'

How could the schoolroom and Miss Wooler's pupils hold her attention when in every unguarded moment the temptation was there to cross the frontier into scenes like these? 'Never shall I, Charlotte Brontë,' she wrote in her journal, 'forget what a voice of wild and wailing music now came thrillingly to my mind's, almost my body's ear, nor how distinctly I, sitting in the school-room at Roe Head, saw the Duke of Zamorna leaning against that obelisk . . . I was quite gone. I had really, utterly forgot where I was, and all the gloom and cheer-lessness of my situation. I felt myself breathing quick and short as I beheld the Duke lifting up his sable crest, which undulated as the plumes of a hearse wave to the wind . . . "Miss Brontë, what are you thinking about?" said a voice, and Miss Lister thrust her little, rough black head into my face.'

Branwell, at home, was as ardently imagining and describing Angrian adventures, and exchanging copious letters on the subject with Charlotte. Word from Branwell that Zamorna had retreated from his burning city and destroyed his palace rather than leave it to the foe, stimulated her more than any actual piece of news from home. 'Last night,' she wrote in reply, 'I did indeed lean upon the thunder-waking wings of such a blast as I have seldom heard blow, and it whirled me away like heath in the wilderness for five seconds of ecstasy; and as I sat by myself in the dining-room while all the rest were at tea, *the trance seemed to descend on a sudden*, and verily this foot trod the war-shaken shores of the Calabar, and these eyes saw the defiled and violated Adrianopolis shedding its lights on the river from lattices whence the invader looked out.'

This imaginative capacity, which in Charlotte seems to have amounted almost to a state of waking trance, was, I believe, still further developed in Emily. Theories to account for the mysterious and unexplainable elements in Emily's genius are familiar bees in every Brontë student's bonnet. They may be said to be almost permanent inhabitants, and put all together would stock a formidable hive. My own interpretation of what has been called the mystical side of Emily's nature is one with which not everyone will agree, but it is perhaps worth considering. I see it as Emily's share in the 'drug-like Brontë dream'; a share more interesting and extraordinary even than Charlotte's, but fundamentally an aspect of the same thing. The strange and unearthly quality of her work, comes, I believe, from the fact that her material was, as Charlotte said, solely 'the vision of her meditations'. Her preoccupation was less with men and women, of whom she knew little, than with God and the soul, with problems of good and evil. Her poems, and her few surviving essays, reveal a mind extraordinarily innocent and independent, an imagination darkened by an aware-ness of evil, free from both sentimentality and optimism. Her view of mankind was, for some reason that we shall never know, profoundly pessimistic; she saw little good in humanity and she expected little; in life, as in her work, she professed no real allegiance to her own kind; she relied upon herself and on her conception of God. The experiences which formed her unique personality are out of our reach: we can never know what they were, or what it was that so early turned her imagination inwards and caused her to refuse the ordinary demands of life, as no doubt she did refuse them. We can only speculate, believing as we now do that some loss of love in childhood, some sense of inadequacy, some fear that love will be refused, are some of the commonest causes of that turning inwards, that refusal of ordinary life which can take many remarkable neurotic forms, and of which Emily Brontë provides a fascinating example. Where there is also genius, as in her case, and a capacity for passion, the mind must discover its own satisfactions, on a secure and private level; and the escape which Emily found in childhood, through the Gondal games, so perfectly answered her imaginative needs that in time it was made to serve her emotionally as well. Her experience, passionate and innocent, lay in a world which she alone controlled, and which was therefore safe. No rebuff, no loss of love could touch her on this level, where she made no demands that she herself could not satisfy. It is from states of mind like this that the recluse, the stoic, and often the hero are made; also the mystic, whose ecstasy lies in sole communion with God; and Emily Brontë contained elements of all these. 'Stronger than a man,' wrote Charlotte 'simpler than a child, her nature stood alone.' The compulsive necessity to rely on herself in everything, on the rest of the world in nothing, was to cause her sisters acute unhappiness at the time of her illness and death; it was also responsible for those mysterious longings which undoubtedly led her into some form of mystical experience.

The word 'mystic' is often so loosely used that it is important to say exactly what we mean when we speak of mystical experience. Briefly, I take it to mean a sense of direct knowledge of or communion with God—Eternity —the Unseen—the Absolute; a state of mind achieved deliberately, with great difficulty, and as a result of considerable self-discipline. It is a state of mind impossible to describe except metaphorically, which is perhaps why mystics of all ages and all creeds have been driven to record their experience in the language of love. It is a process and a means of ecstasy so rare that it has never evolved a language of its own. It is a form of trance; there is a partial suspension of consciousness not unlike that experienced in hypnosis, but it differs from other forms of self-induced trance in that it has a mounting ecstasy and crisis, and there is often considerable distress as consciousness returns. The emotion at its peak is one of spiritual exaltation, usually expressed in terms of union and love; indeed it cannot be described otherwise; and it is possible to maintain that the experience is closer to that of sexual love than many people are willing to believe.

Mystical experience is not necessarily religious, though it is usually associated with religious emotion, even among those primitive peoples who achieve their ecstasies through fasting or the use of drugs. It seems always to follow the same course, through meditation and concentration and what St Theresa of Avila calls 'the sleep of the mental faculties,' to the final ecstasy; and it is interesting to compare St Theresa's own account with Emily Brontë's. 'The soul,' wrote St Theresa, describing

27

the ecstasy, 'seems to leave the organs which she animates . . . she falls into a sort of swoon . . . It is only with the greatest effort that she can make the slightest movement with her hands. The eyes close of themselves, and if they are kept open, they see almost nothing . . . If spoken to, the soul hears the sound of the voice, but no distinct word.' This state is evidently very close to that self-induced hypnotic state which many types of people are able to achieve, either spontaneously or after learning a technique; it implies a degree of mental and physical relaxation so complete that consciousness becomes extremely thin, or is suspended altogether, and if the conscious emotions at the moment of entering trance are concentrated on the idea of spiritual union with God, or with some force greater than self, the adept is occasionally able to reach rapture. There seems no doubt that Emily Brontë, alone at night in the little closet-like bedroom which had once been the children's study and was now her securest retreat, did achieve something of the same experience, though her account of it—marvellously expressive and perhaps the closest description of mystical experience that we have—does not precisely identify the union achieved as being with God. The Unseen, the Invisible, a messenger of Hope—she avoids the conventional religious terms, and seems to feel that the spirit of her communion is too huge and abstract to be pinned down by any name.

The wonderful poem describing the mystical ecstasy, like nearly all of Emily's that survive, is embedded in the Gondal mass and does not stand alone. There is nothing to suggest that it describes Emily's own experience, except that the famous stanzas beginning, 'He comes with

western winds, with evening's wandering airs,' leap
suddenly to life in the midst of pages of Gondal verse on a
very pedestrian level. There is a force, a ring of truth
about them which make it very difficult to accept them as
purely invented for one of the Gondal heroines: and the
poem describes a spiritual adventure so rare that it seems
unlikely to have been inspired by anything less real than
inner knowledge. My own belief is that it describes the
peak of Emily's experience of the 'drug-like Brontë
dream,' in which, in their different ways, they all shared.

It now remains to consider Branwell's manifestation of
it, and what little we know of Anne's. Branwell's tragedy
is much more easily understood in the light of this
imaginative obsession, this turning away from real life
and preferring to dwell in a sort of opium dream which
was more satisfying than reality. The unbearable reality
from which Branwell sought relief was the fact that he
could never fulfil his apparently brilliant promise. He
possessed to an extreme degree that kind of temperament
which collapses under pressure. Like many a seeming
genius, he found the test of performance impossible to
face because nothing he could ever do could reach the
expected standard. Poor Branwell's unhappy career is
starred with failures; he became obsessed with failure to a
degree unknown to those who have never been under a
comparable pressure towards success; and desperately
cast about for ways of escape. The means of escape were
not many, but there were a few; and among them were the
illusions of drink and opium.

Drunkenness was very common in all classes in
Branwell's youth, even in Yorkshire, and we all know that
whisky was Mr Brontë's secret weakness. It was fatally

easy for the boy, idle and tormented by his own ambitions and inadequacies, to comfort himself with drink. But drink was not enough. Branwell lacked the imaginative power of Charlotte and Emily; he could not produce his drug, as they did, out of his own mind; to escape into a sufficiently strong illusion he had to resort to opium. I think a great many people have been far too shocked by Branwell's taking to opium in his twenties. They forget how easily, in his time, anyone could buy laudanum—which is simply a solution of opium in alcohol—for a few pence, without anybody thinking anything of it. De Quincey and Coleridge had made it fashionable among literary men, and it was more than that—it was in universal use as a domestic remedy. No sensible person endured a toothache or neuralgia if they could get it, doctors freely prescribed it, even for children; it was, indeed, the nineteenth-century equivalent of the aspirin. Branwell may very easily have come to it first as a simple remedy, and have been drawn gradually into habitual use as he discovered its effects, which to his unstable nature were particularly attractive.

The effect of laudanum is not, apparently, erotic. It seems, on the contrary, to produce very often an illusion of intellectual brilliance in which everything is clear and everything possible. It offers special rewards to the writer and artist because the dreams it induces remain in waking memory; they are accessible to the conscious mind and so are a source of imaginative material. It is apparently able, too, to compose a harassed and despairing mind and induce a delicious temporary tranquillity, full of confidence. 'You, I believe,' wrote Coleridge to his brother, 'know how divine that repose is, what a spot of enchantment, a green spot of fountain and flowers and trees in the very heart of a waste of sands.' It is small wonder that Branwell, as the years went by and it became ever more mercilessly clear that he would never fulfil his early promise, should take refuge in this friendly drug which gave him the illusion of mastery over his unmanageable world.

Unfortunately we know very little about Anne. I see her, as she has been described, as 'a Brontë without genius,' but as one who certainly had her share of the Brontë temperament. She too, I believe, unconsciously turned away from ordinary life, and dwelt instead in a dream of her own making. The day-dreams that people substitute for reality are not always happy ones, as anyone who has had any experience of mental illness will tell you. For one hallucinated patient who has happy visions there are always ten who are haunted by dreams of anxiety and fear. I am not, of course, suggesting that Anne Brontë was hallucinated; but the religious melancholy from which she suffered, the tragic conviction of her unworthiness of God's love which speaks so plainly in her poems, suggests to me that she suffered the same loss of love in childhood that Emily did—perhaps the loss of their mother—and that it injured her as, with very different and wonderful results, it injured Emily. Anne's tragedy seems to me to lie in her unconscious choice of a particularly uncomforting religion as the mental drug with which she sought to make life bearable. I am convinced it was as much a part of the 'drug-like Brontë dream' as the Gondal legends that she shared with Emily—an imaginative resource so powerful that it had the quality of vision. It is this quality of vision, seen with all the intensity of the real, which is

the true source and secret of the Brontë genius—the
mysterious difference which gives Charlotte and Emily
their unique place in our literature.

2

The Brontës in the Schoolroom

2

The Brontës in the Schoolroom

WHEN I ENVISAGE the Brontës in the schoolroom I am thinking, of course, of Charlotte and Emily. Their brother Branwell never went to school; he was taught entirely by their father. Anne Brontë had a brief experience of Miss Wooler's school at Roe Head and was afterwards a governess for a much longer period than Charlotte. But Charlotte was the one on whom, as a writer, the experience of school and education was quite extraordinarily influential.

Emily, I think, was beyond the reach of influence even from her earliest days; but she did pass through, briefly, Cowan Bridge School, Miss Wooler's, and the one at Law Hill, and spent nine months in Brussels in Madame Heger's establishment. Her imaginative development during all that period went on in secret, as though in a cell shut off from the outside world; and I propose to deal with that separately.

If we consider Charlotte Brontë's life as a whole, it is extraordinary how much of it is concerned with the schoolroom. I use the word 'schoolroom' in a broad sense, to cover not only Charlotte's own experience of it, both as pupil and teacher, and her response to the master-pupil relationship, but also her lifelong concern with the whole subject of education—learning, reading, literature, art, the magic which fed and nourished her imagination.

This passionate concern with education was common to all the Brontës. Mr Brontë himself was a classic example of the poor Irish peasant, son of practically illiterate parents, who by sheer force of intelligence had managed to get to Cambridge, to take Holy Orders, and to end up as a respected Yorkshire clergyman. Both he and his wife had a veneration for learning which they passed on to all their children. Charlotte's obsession with the subject is the most striking—three out of her four novels are about teachers, pupils and schools, and even the unfinished fragment she was writing when she died takes us at once into a schoolroom with an unhappy pupil—a scene so close to her earlier work that her husband, Mr Nicholls, warned her the critics would accuse her of repetition.

As Charlotte herself repeatedly reminded her publishers, her own experience of life was extremely narrow: in writing of schools and governesses she was writing only of what she knew: this was the world in which she had known both happiness and suffering. But there was more to it than that; there was both attraction and repulsion in the subject, and the intensity of her knowledge of this sphere was such that her words reach us as a heart-cry, a personal message.

What was the world of the schoolroom like then, for girls, in the first quarter of the nineteenth century? What sort of education were they given, how did they profit by it? By modern standards it was pretty lamentable. A meagre and haphazard amount of teaching was considered quite good enough for girls, and nobody thought it strange if they went without. Religious instruction and needlework were essential, if you had any pretension to gentility; reading and writing came next in importance, and the rudiments of arithmetic. All this, in a sketchy fashion, could be given at home if the parents had time,

and this do-it-yourself sort of education, bad or middling, was the fate of most girls when Charlotte Brontë was old enough to learn anything.

Only the children of gentlefolk had any pretensions at all to real education. A poor child was just as likely to be put to work in the mines, or in a spinning mill, or just left to grow up haphazard at home or in the streets, or at best to be taught to read and write in a ragged school or some charitable institution. (It is worth remembering that when Charlotte Brontë went to her first situation as governess in 1839, to the children of Mrs Sidgwick at Stonegappe near Skipton, it wasn't long since the children employed in the Sidgwicks' own spinning mill had been working thirteen hours a day.) There were innumerable small schools for girls, as there had been since the eighteenth century, but they had no standard of education, and for the most part were either places where children were sent to be out of the way, or else so-called establishments where young ladies were finished. The best, I dare say, were probably the least pretentious, the little schools of a dozen pupils, like Mrs Goddard's in Jane Austen's *Emma*, which 'was not a seminary, or an establishment . . . but a real honest old-fashioned boarding-school, where a reasonable quantity of accomplishments were sold at a reasonable price, and where girls might be sent to be out of the way, and scramble themselves into a little education, without any danger of coming back prodigies.'

For the girl who was educated at home, there was one almost universal key to knowledge, Miss Richmal Mangnall's *Historical and Miscellaneous Questions*. Miss Mangnall was a Yorkshire schoolteacher, and this book made her famous. It is made up of lists of facts and endless question and answer, and in a period when education consisted largely of learning by rote I suppose it was better than nothing, since some of the scraps would stick. But as a system of education it leaves much to be desired. This, for instance, in an old copy which has somehow survived in my family, is the whole of the entry under William Shakespeare: 'Born in Warwickshire, 1564; died, 1616. The Poet of Nature, Fancy's Child. His plays have been edited by Rowe, Pope, Theobald, Sir Thomas Hammer, Dr Warburton, Mr Capell, Mr Stevens, and Dr Johnson with notes.'

Charlotte and Emily Brontë certainly knew Mangnall's Questions; they were a standard piece of equipment in any home where there were children to be educated; but I doubt whether they were thought very much of at Haworth Parsonage. There, until four of the five sisters were sent to Cowan Bridge School, Mr Brontë was in the habit of setting them a task in the morning, and leaving them to get on with it for a specified period, under the supervision, one supposes, of their Aunt Branwell. The beauty of this system for these particular children—especially after the Cowan Bridge period, when Charlotte and Emily were old enough to benefit from it—was that they had the free run of all the books in the house, their father's included, and of such magazines and periodicals as Mr Brontë subscribed to, exactly as though they were grown-ups and on the same intellectual level as their father. For children bookish by nature, and inheriting, as the Brontës did, an extraordinary imagination and intellectual curiosity, there is nothing so stimulating as being allowed to read everything in sight—books, newspapers, magazines, whatever comes to hand—but it doesn't produce a conventional education, and we know that when Charlotte at eight years old was sent to the Clergy Daughters' School at Cowan Bridge, the report on her achievements was not encouraging—'Knows nothing of grammar, geography, history or accomplishments—altogether clever of her age but knows nothing systematically.' Emily, at six, rated rather better: 'Reads very prettily and works'—that is to say, sews—'a little'.

Everyone who has read *Jane Eyre* knows how appalling the experience of Cowan Bridge proved to be. After the publication of Mrs Gaskell's *Life* there was a fierce outcry in certain quarters against the clearly recognisable account which Charlotte had given of the Rev. Carus Wilson's charitable school. And there is no doubt that after the school had been moved and its management improved, it was a great deal better than it was in the beginning. But the evidence against Cowan Bridge is overwhelming. Mr Carus Wilson's motives looked well in print, but he was a type of man who should never have been allowed to have control of a school, let alone young children. I tremble to think what a scandal a modern Cowan Bridge would provoke today. One remembers the cold, and the suffering from chilblains; the insufficient clothing in winter, the thin shoes that soaked up the snow on the long walk to church, and the endless waits in damp clothing between services; the disgusting food that was never enough to go round, the burnt porridge, the harshness of the discipline, the punishments inflicted on Helen Burns, who, like Charlotte's own sisters, Maria and Elizabeth, was dying of consumption. And as for Carus Wilson himself, I think anyone who has read his books for children can see only too clearly the neurotic obsessed with power, going about his work with all the zeal of the unconscious sadist. Mr Wilson's God was one whose Hell was always full, especially of children, and in following Him he served a Deity very much like himself. It was bad luck that at the beginning he had among the Clergy Daughters an abnormally quiet child of eight who would never forgive him.

If anyone thinks that Charlotte exaggerated when she described the school in *Jane Eyre*, I would remind them of two actual details which speak volumes. One is, that six girls died of tuberculosis during the few months that the Brontë sisters were at the school, quite apart from the numbers who died in the typhoid epidemic of the same year: and the other, that the sanitary arrangements consisted of one outdoor privy, shared between seventy persons, which makes the deaths from typhoid under-standable.

Fortunately for Charlotte and Emily, Mr Brontë removed them as soon as he realised that this charitable school, which had seemed such a godsend to a poor curate, was nothing but a death-trap; and took them back to Haworth: but in the case of the elder two, Maria and Elizabeth, he was too late. Tragedies of this sort always make one marvel afresh at the silences of children. Why hadn't they written home, and told their father that the misery was unbearable? Their letters were censored, of course, but there's a deeper reason. Children, like primitive people, accept what comes with a kind of un-questioning fatalism, having no means of comparison. The hurts of childhood can last a lifetime, and Charlotte Brontë certainly, from this first experience of a real schoolroom, never lost her obsession with that defenceless self which finds itself at the mercy of callous strangers.

Fortunately though, for Charlotte and her surviving sisters, the six years following the Cowan Bridge disaster were the happiest in their lives. There was no more talk of school for any of them, not even Branwell. The rather haphazard home lessons continued, and because books and reading played a dominating part in their games and pleasures, they were soon embarked on that extraordinary secret career of invention and book-making, which is one of the strangest features in the whole history of the Brontës.

The famous 'plays' that engrossed them were not, of course, a unique phenomenon. Many imaginative children go through this phase at some stage, and many of us can remember make-believe sagas which were played out with brothers and sisters and which went on for years. Robert Louis Stevenson, for instance, as a small boy in Edinburgh with his cousins, had a series of imaginary plays which were very like the Brontës'. 'We lived together,' he wrote afterwards, 'in a purely visionary state. We had countries . . . where we ruled and made wars and inventions, and . . . maps . . . We were never weary of dressing up.' We never hear of the Brontës dressing up: I don't imagine there was a dressing-up box at the Parsonage, where every garment would be carefully darned and turned and finally cut up for something useful. The extraordinary feature about *their* sagas was that they were turned into literary material as fast as they were invented. The things they wrote even had to *look* like books, while the secrecy of their contents was preserved by their tiny size. I know of no more extraordinary apprenticeship to the literary life than this vast childhood production; and I suppose it could have happened in no other environment—five years of freedom from the schoolroom, of comparative independence, of self-education and self-amusement, the perfect forcing-ground for these particular children at that particular age.

But in 1831, when Charlotte was nearly fifteen, the shadow of the schoolroom once more looms ahead, and the blissful period is over. Mr Brontë, who had done better than he knew in leaving the children largely to their own devices, became alarmed about his health, and realised that, if anything should happen to him, the children must be able to earn their living. Branwell he would continue to teach himself, giving him a good classical grounding, and Charlotte, the eldest, since her godparents were willing to pay, was to be sent for a second time to a strange school.

Luckily, this one was as different from Cowan Bridge as chalk from cheese. Miss Wooler's school at Roe Head sounds very much like that other comfortable one that we've glanced at before, in Jane Austen's *Emma*. There were only ten boarders, so there was plenty of room and individual attention, and Miss Wooler and her three sisters were kind, and quite reasonably well educated and capable. There is no doubt that Charlotte benefited greatly from the three half-years she spent there as a boarder. In the first place, she made two lifelong friends, Ellen Nussey and Mary Taylor, whose importance in her life, as objects of love and sharers of confidences, can scarcely be exaggerated. And Miss Wooler eventually became a trusted friend, whose example profoundly influenced Charlotte's thoughts on the subject of unmarried women. And as well as these admirable friends, who were to last her lifetime,

Charlotte began for the first time to work along conventional educational lines, and at the end of her first half
bore off the three main prizes. She must, in spite of her
short-sightedness and her hopelessness at games, have
been a wonderful pupil to have in the school, the sort that
ambitious teachers dream of. And indeed, in all her
schoolroom life, both as a child and as a young grown-up,
it was to the role of pupil to which Charlotte's temperament responded. But even at Miss Wooler's I doubt if she
was ever *happy*, for school itself meant the loss of that
marvellous freedom she had enjoyed, and the secret
creative partnership with Branwell, which had meant so
much. How wonderful it must have seemed to her when,
at sixteen, she left Miss Wooler's, as she believed, for good,
and flew back to those creative excitements with Branwell
and her sisters, which were the real centre of her life! I
believe we are often tempted to think of Charlotte
Brontë's life as a story painfully sad from beginning to
end, but at least there were these two utterly happy periods,
both before and after her experience as a pupil at Roe
Head, when she had love and freedom and the intoxication
of creative expression such as few writers ever experience
in youth. What it had meant to her, and the violent and
hallucinated hold it had on her, we know when her life
changed *again* when she was just nineteen, and she found
herself back at Miss Wooler's, and again in the schoolroom.

Now she was earning her living, or at least her younger
sisters' education, for Emily was briefly a pupil there, and
then Anne, while Charlotte was a teacher. This was
something, she found, which was against the very grain
of her nature. Of all professions—and the bitterness was,

44

it was the only one open to her—teaching was the very
one calculated to cause her the most wretchedness. In a
later period, perhaps if she had lived somewhere nearer
our own time, she might have borne it better, for even
teachers today are allowed some freedom and leisure, and
nobody thinks it right that they should be drudges.
Charlotte was already set on the course that was to make
her a great writer, and leisure, and quiet, and freedom of
mind, those great essentials, were now denied her. Her
private journal at this time, and her letters to Branwell,
make painful reading. The intensity with which, even
when on duty in the classroom, she reverted to their
private world of passion and adventure, suggests that she
actually, like Emily, experienced some kind of trance;
that she was capable to a rare degree of hallucination or
self-hypnosis; that she saw things, with her eyes open,
which were invisible to others, that she could lose herself
as completely as a trance medium.

That is by no means the temperament for a schoolteacher, but it was perhaps fortunate for women teachers
as a whole, and particularly for governesses in private
families, that Charlotte Brontë for some part of her life
was one of them, and spoke with such an eloquent voice of
the inhumanities of their situation. Most people today
have forgotten about governesses, so few of them have
survived into the space age; but I can remember one or
two of my contemporaries considering it a great point of
superiority never to have been at school, but always to
have had a governess, and in the preceding generation
governesses were plentiful. The few that I remember, in
the families of childhood friends, were almost indisting-
uishable from aunts, and the relationship was very easy;

but a hundred years earlier, when Charlotte went to her first situation, the governess was treated, at best as a humble dependant, and often with less consideration than the servants.

It is rather curious, in view of the importance of the governess theme in Charlotte's novels, that she herself was one for rather less than a year—two months with the Sidgwicks and nine with the Whites at Rawdon. Her misery, especially during the Sidgwick spell, must have been acute, to have made such a very bitter and lasting impression. 'I have striven hard to be pleased with my new situation', she wrote to Emily, 'but alack-a-day! there is such a thing as seeing all things beautiful around you ... and not having a free moment or a free thought left to enjoy them in. The children are constantly with me, and more riotous, perverse, unmanageable cubs never grew. As for correcting them, I soon found that that was entirely out of the question: they are to do as they like.' And she goes on: 'I said in my last letter that Mrs Sidgwick did not know me. I now begin to find that she does not intend to know me, that she cares nothing in the world about me except to contrive how the greatest possible quantity of labour may be squeezed out of me, and to that end she overwhelms me with needlework, yards of cambric to hem, muslin nightcaps to make, and above all things, dolls to dress. I do not think she likes me at all, and ... I see now more clearly than I have ever done before that a private governess has no existence, is not considered as a living and rational being, except as connected with the wearisome duties she has to fulfill.'

Clearly the situation was unsatisfactory on both sides. Charlotte, with all her marvellous gifts, was shy and difficult among strangers, not really good with children, and I suspect touchy. If she had been with a different type of family, with people of good breeding, she would have fared better, for as we know, the governess's lot *could* be a happy one. Charlotte Young, who knew far more about them as a whole than Charlotte did, said, 'Insolence to a governess is a stock complaint, but in real life I never heard of it from anyone by birth and breeding a lady.' Mrs Sidgwick obviously wasn't a lady, and it was Charlotte Brontë's bad luck that, in that period and that part of Yorkshire, the jobs that were going were with families of the *nouveau riche* manufacturing class who were on their way up in the world and hadn't had time to achieve agreeable manners. I don't believe that Charlotte exaggerated a bit, either in *Jane Eyre* or in her letters. There are one or two little telling phrases that one never forgets— Mr Sidgwick, for instance, whom she rather liked, walking out with his children, and giving Miss Brontë orders to 'follow a little behind', and Mrs Sidgwick's famous exclamation when one of the smaller children said, 'I love 'ou, Miss Brontë'—'Love the *governess*, my dear?' Charlotte's experience, too, was reinforced by Anne's, which was much longer; Anne was a private governess for nearly six years, and what *she* thought of it we know well enough from the pages of *Agnes Grey*. As Charlotte told Mrs Gaskell, 'None but those who had been in the position of a governess could ever realise the dark side of "respectable" human nature.'

There is plenty of evidence from other sources to dispose of the idea that Charlotte exaggerated, and the conversation of Lady Ingram in *Jane Eyre*, so often mocked, I am quite sure is true to life, and as faithful a transcript of what went on as if Charlotte Brontë had had a tape-recorder under her needlework. Yet, in spite of all, when she had finally escaped from the Sidgwicks and the Whites and was at home again, it was still to the schoolroom that she looked for independence—not the so-called schoolroom of a private household—'I hate and abhor the very thought of governesship,' she wrote violently to Ellen Nussey—but their own, in the 'Miss Brontës Establishment for the Board and Education of a Limited Number of Young Ladies'.

It was all going to be entirely different, and one wonders what it would have been like, if it had come to pass. Where would they have put the young ladies, in the very small house that the Parsonage was in those days? How would Mr Brontë have liked it, when the place was full of great girls? And would he have been allowed to keep the parlour, which was his private domain? Was it he, perhaps, who was prepared to give those Latin lessons at an extra guinea a quarter? We shall never know, since the Misses Brontës' Establishment never materialised; and sad though this was at the time, perhaps it was as well, for a busy headmistress, occupied from morning till night, as she would have been, would never have written *Jane Eyre* and *Villette*, *Shirley* and *The Professor*. As it was, by another repeat of this curious pattern which took Charlotte Brontë in and out of schoolrooms for the greater part of her life, we find her next with Emily in Brussels, pupils once more, seriously striving to improve their qualifications for the great undertaking of their school, but in fact approaching the major emotional experience of Charlotte's life.

It is somehow mysteriously appropriate that Charlotte

Brontë's one great falling in love should have been in a
schoolroom, and her finest achievement, *Villette*, the fruit
of a most intense master-pupil relationship. It was
perhaps inevitable that she should have fallen in love with
M. Heger, and equally inevitable that she should not
have realised for ages what was happening. For the first
time she was in a professionally conducted, highly reput-
able school, working under a master of exceptional
brilliance. There is no doubt whatever that Constantin
Heger had a genius for teaching, that he could fire a
responsive pupil to perform prodigies, and that he himself
was immensely stimulated by a pupil's enthusiasm. There
is also no doubt that, deeply respectable married man
though he was, serious Catholic, good husband and father,
he possessed that kind of personal dynamism which
simply cannot help responding to admiration. There was
certainly an exchange of magnetism between him and
Charlotte, and, I suspect, between him and certain other
young ladies. In Winifred Gerin's biography of Charlotte
there are two letters of M. Heger's to a former pupil
which I do not remember having seen before. This other
English girl had evidently enjoyed the sort of affectionate
exchange of letters that Charlotte yearned for, and his
letters show him to have been a most attractive correspond-
ent, skilled in subtle emotional exchanges. There is
another very interesting detail, too, in Dr Phyllis Bentley's
pictorial biography, *The Brontës and their World*. In this,
there is reproduced a most eloquent painting of the whole
Heger family, done four or five years after Charlotte's time
in Brussels. It has been reproduced before, but never so
well, and in fact, as Dr Bentley points out, there has been
a conspiracy of invisibility about M. Heger until recently,

and the only portraits that English readers were allowed to see were of him in middle-age, or even bald old age, looking like an archbishop, a piece of discretion that would certainly have been approved by Mrs Gaskell. But *this* portrait shows him as Charlotte knew him, in his thirties, and extremely fascinating and attractive. Such a master in any school was bound to inspire crushes and more lasting attachments: *that* we can see from the portrait: and for his intellectual as well as physical magnetism we have only to turn to *Villette*, and Charlotte's marvellously living creation of Paul Emmanuel.

That long, unhappy and hopeless love of hers for M. Heger is something I find almost too painful to dwell on. Her surviving letters to him after she left Brussels, when as she confessed, for two years she forfeited all peace of mind, still throb with a pain which makes us wince as we read. But in a sense it was the beginning of the destiny she had all along been preparing for; and soon the obsessive schoolroom theme was to put out roots and leaves, and the unloved child, the friendless governess, the drama of master and pupil were to come to light in *Jane Eyre*, in *The Professor*, in *Villette*.

Emily's experience during her few months in Brussels was very different. Her intellect impressed M. Heger more than Charlotte's, but he found her egotistical and exacting, not easy to teach. As Charlotte wrote in a letter, 'Emily and he don't draw well together at all.' But what was happening to Emily Brontë in that Brussels school-room was that withdrawal into herself, that fierce refusal of any but her own spiritual nourishment, which had come to a crisis every time that she had been taken away from home. M. Heger could not know this, but Emily, instead of concentrating on his theories, was composing poetry which belonged to her own inner world, and which nobody has so far managed to explain.

Here, of course, we approach the brink of that perilous question—what *happened* to Emily Brontë? What was the private wound she suffered? What traumatic experience in childhood or youth gave rise to that secrecy and pessimism, drove her into stoical resistance as to a stronghold, fortified and obsessed by an impenetrable inner life?

> So hopeless is the world without,
> The world within I doubly prize . . .

And again,

> O, in the days of ardent youth
> I would have given my life for truth.

But youth is no longer ardent, it is past, even at nineteen or twenty.

> My breast still braves the world alone,
> Steeled as it ever was to terror.

Of what? We are not told.

> No sighs for me, no sympathy,
> No wish to keep my soul below;
> The heart is dead since infancy;
> Unwept-for let the body go.

But what had the heart died of? She does not say. She is not asking for pity. But the cryptic utterances and unanswered questions remain, and I shall resist the temptation to try and astonish the world with a new theory.

After the death of Emily, Branwell, and finally Anne,

Charlotte was indeed alone, bereft of the two sisters who had always meant so much. She was neither pupil nor teacher now, and had only an excess of that leisure and freedom to create that she had always longed for. It was a bleak and lonely outlook, that solitary life in Haworth, and she faced it with a sinking heart and admirable courage. 'I speculate much,' she wrote to Miss Wooler, 'on the existence of unmarried and never-to-be-married women nowadays, and I have already got to the point of considering that there is no more respectable character on this earth than an unmarried women who makes her own way through life quietly, perseveringly, without support of husband or brother, and who, having attained the age of 45 or upwards, retains in her possession a well regulated mind, a disposition to enjoy simple pleasure, fortitude to support inevitable pains, sympathy with the sufferings of others, and willingness to relieve want as far as her means extend.'

How grateful one is, brooding on this period of Charlotte's life and its melancholy undertones, for that period of comparative happiness that comes before the end. I have always been rather fond of Mr Nicholls, for all his shortcomings, and it strikes me as charmingly appropriate that Charlotte's respect and affection for him, during their honeymoon, should have taken a distinct leap forward in an Irish schoolroom. She had approached the marriage in a very unenthusiastic, almost resigned, frame of mind. 'I am very calm,' she told Ellen Nussey, 'very inexpectant. What I taste of happiness is of the soberest order. I trust to love my husband . . . I believe him to be an affectionate, a conscientious, a high-principled man; and if, with all this, I should yield to regrets, that fine talents, congenial tastes and thoughts are not added, it seems to me I should be most presumptuous and thankless.' A sadly sober and making-the-best-of-a-bad-job tone for a bride! But when, on their honeymoon, they reached Banagher, that unknown spot in King's County that Mr Nicholls came from, there was a perceptible change. They were received into Cuba House, the home of Mr Nicholls's uncle, the late Dr Bell, and Charlotte found herself among charming people and in congenial surroundings—very different, one suspects, from what she had feared and expected. And Cuba House, where Mr Nicholls had been brought up as a boy, was—how wonderful!—a school; and it was a handsome house and the educational standards were high, and Dr Bell's son James was headmaster, and there were long airy class-rooms and excellent dormitories. It must have been like a dream (for term was over and the pupils on holiday), and I cannot at all agree with those critics who put down Charlotte's change of heart about her 'dear Arthur' to the fact that she found that he came from a country house and that his relations were gentlefolk. Naturally that played its part; it would be unrealistic to discount it; but I also believe that to walk into that old familiar atmosphere, breathing that chalk and classroom smell which was like a breath of childhood, bringing back lost days of happiness and suffering, and hope and aspiration, did more to make Charlotte feel at home, and reassure her, than the sight of the carriage drive and table silver. The schoolroom had played an extraordinary part in her life, and she had spoken with one of the most eloquent voices of the century of the experience, both painful and inspired, that it had given her.

On Emily, I think, it left no mark at all. She had withdrawn from it, like an animal retreating from danger into a secret burrow, where her imaginative life went on, detached from the outside world. But Charlotte, quite apart from the literary achievement of her novels, had contributed something else to the progress of her own time. There could never be another Cowan Bridge since she had created Lowood, and in the never-to-be-forgotten voice of Jane Eyre the private governess had uttered her indignation.

If I had anything to do with a school, I would have Charlotte Brontë's portrait on the wall, as well as the maps and the blackboard. And perhaps a picture of Mr Nicholls too, and even one of M. Heger in the staff-room. Though even today that might not be quite approved of. . . .

3
Emily Brontë in a Cold Climate

3

Emily Brontë in a Cold Climate

SOME YEARS AGO, when I was going out to East Africa to spend a month or so in a remote part of what was then called Tanganyika, I decided—since I guessed that books would be few in the bush and time might hang heavily—to pack my pocket editions of Jane Austen, and to read all her novels again, as though, if that were possible, for the first time. I did so, and spent many contented afternoons in the heat and the long grass, considering Elizabeth Bennett and Emma Woodhouse, Mr Darcy and Mr Knightley and the rest, in these strange surroundings. The contrast couldn't have been more complete, and it seemed to me as I went on that the experiment was working. I noticed points and made small discoveries that had escaped me before, and I ended up so struck with one aspect of Jane Austen's art that I had so far missed—I mean her ability to create an almost visible scene or interior without, or almost without, the aid of description—that I finally relieved my feelings by writing about it.

Recently I tried to repeat the experiment, this time with Emily Brontë, and the attempt was a failure. I went out in February, to the same place, the same alien and solitary conditions, fondly supposing that if I read *Wuthering Heights* and a selection of the poems—again, I intended, as though for the first time—my mind would be so open and undistracted that a ray of light might penetrate some of the mysteries, that I might see just a hand's breadth further into the working of genius. It was not so,

not at all. In that strange and wild setting—and this time
the rains had arrived, and there were huge storms, with
rain drumming and vibrating on the tin roof—Emily
Brontë, both in prose and verse, became unbearable. The
Yorkshire moors were a foreign country, and the atmosphere too frightening. There was a bird that called
incessantly whenever the rain stopped, the bush-cuckoo
or coucal, which Africans call the brain-fever bird,
believing it can drive men mad; and I caught, as Emily
Brontë would have said, a fever, and my dreams were
frightful. In my dark bedroom, which I shared, most
unwillingly, with a tribe of cockroaches, the nightmare or
bad-dream quality of *Wuthering Heights*, which is a
part of its fascination, became too insufferably oppressive,
and I had to put the book aside. Heathcliff had a Dracula
quality; he was 'a ghoul, an afreet', as Charlotte Brontë
saw him, and the familiar world of northern nature, so
wonderfully evoked in the novel, with its storms and snow
and sudden spring-like mornings, 'the whole world
awake and wild with joy', was something I couldn't
imagine. It was at once too powerful, too difficult; it
didn't *work* in those African conditions, or it worked
diabolically; and it wasn't until I got home again, and the
climate, without and within, was northern and normal,
that I was able to plunge back into *Wuthering Heights* and
to receive those signals from outer space which apparently, and so disturbingly, emanate from Emily Brontë.

The whole experience reminded me of that essay of
Aldous Huxley's, on *Wordsworth in the Tropics*, in which
he makes the point that Wordsworth's worship of nature
as something beneficent and noble, having a mysterious
kinship with man, whom it protects and comforts, doesn't

really survive transplantation to a tropical climate, and that those who think of Nature as a kindly nurse are often mistaken. The Wordsworthian type of nature-worship, in fact, is possible only, he says, 'for those who are prepared to falsify their immediate intuitions of Nature. For Nature, even in the temperate zone, is always alien and inhuman, and occasionally diabolic.' Was this, I wondered, why I had not been able to read Emily Brontë within sight of those swamps and forests and the Ruvuma River? Did her attitude to Nature, in those conditions, ring slightly false? For Emily Brontë was essentially an out-door person; we do not need to be reminded how power-ful a part the elements play in the poems and in *Wuthering Heights*. So vital, indeed, are her brief passages on weather and terrain (and if you have forgotten how brief they are, remember the descriptions of scenery and weather in Sir Walter Scott) that I am surprised no American professor has written a thesis to prove that the weather is the real villain in *Wuthering Heights*, or that Cathy's preference for lying in a cradle of branches on a windy day is an anagram of sexual symbolism.

No; on the contrary, it is partly because Emily Brontë does *not* falsify her intuitions of Nature, or in any sense attempt to humanise the natural world, that the atmo-sphere of *Wuthering Heights* is so compelling. The elements are not concerned with man, but man—or at least that aspect that we see in Heathcliff and Catherine, and in Emily Brontë herself—is concerned to the point of identity with the elements. And here in Aldous Huxley's essay, which I turned to the other day to remind myself of what he had said, I found this sentence, which seemed now to stand up from the page, so clearly did it point to Emily Brontë: 'Our direct intuitions of Nature tell us that the world is bottomlessly strange; alien, even when it is kind and beautiful; having innumerable modes of being that are not our modes; always mysteriously not personal, not conscious, not moral; often hostile and sinister; sometimes even unimaginably, because inhumanly, evil.' There is so much in this long sentence that is in tune with the ideas that one receives from *Wuthering Heights*, with the suggestions and intimations that seem always to be stirring below the surface, that I find it uncanny. The novel itself is 'bottomlessly strange'; it hints at 'modes of being that are not our modes'; has a tone of voice 'not personal, not conscious, not moral'; there are influences abroad in it which to many people have seemed 'unimaginably, because inhumanly, evil'. I am led to believe that Emily Brontë, like Wordsworth, is best read in a cold climate.

Emily Brontë's mode of being, indeed, is not our mode, and there are things in her work which are bottomlessly strange; yet there are also things in her great novel and in a few of the trivial facts that we know about her, that are so solid and familiar, we feel we ought to understand everything about her—and that is dangerous. Those wonderful farmhouse interiors at Wuthering Heights, the blazing fires in winter and summer (still necessary in the north, or at least desirable), the pewter dishes on the dresser reflecting heat as well as light, the flagged floor white with scrubbing, the wooden table, the oatcakes, the smoking porridge—all described with a domestic lyricism that is like a personal memory to anyone born in the north. And those few glimpses that we have of Emily herself in her domestic occupations: doing the baking, 'pilling a potate', mixing her dough with a book propped open before her, picking blackcurrants in the garden or eating her breakfast porridge with Anne and letting the dogs have the last of it—it is all so normal and homely, so familiar and secure, that when she sits with her box-desk on her knee in the dining-room, and there is the sound of three pens scratching, we feel we should understand what is going on there as well, the thoughts that are driving that difficult and secretive handwriting. Even when she is alone, in that little closet of a bedroom, and leans at the open window, gazing at the night, even here, when the lines of a poem are taking shape, we feel that we ought to understand what it is all about, that the experience giving rise to the words must be somehow *explicable*. And very often, to our confusion, it is not. The words are simple, they are melancholy and moving, but what is behind them? And we begin to speculate. We cannot help it; it is irresistible; we are rational creatures and we like to have a clear idea of what is going on. But to try to pin Emily Brontë down is as difficult to-day as ever it was; perhaps more so; and almost invariably delusive. No writer in the whole of our literature has driven critics and scholars into such ingenious absurdities.

Whenever I read some of the learned theories about *Wuthering Heights*, I am reminded of that scene in the dining-room at the Parsonage, when, as we know from Charlotte, Emily read the finished manuscript aloud to her sisters. 'If the auditor,' said Charlotte, who clearly had done this very thing, 'shuddered under the grinding influence of natures so relentless and implacable, of spirits so lost and fallen; if it was complained that the mere hearing of certain vivid and fearful scenes banished

sleep by night, and disturbed mental peace by day, Ellis
Bell would wonder what was meant, and suspect the
complainant of affectation.' And that later occasion in the
same room, when *Wuthering Heights* had been published,
and a reviewer had described the author as 'a man of
uncommon talents, but dogged, brutal and morose', we
remember that Emily, then not far from death, 'smiled
half amused and half in scorn' as she listened. With what
amusement, I wonder, or what scorn, would she read
some of the theories and analyses of today! The palm, I
fancy, would go to America, where the literary criticism
industry turns out some marvellously strange examples of
Brontë theory. My own favourite, of the How-Absurd-
Can-You-Get school, is that professor from Washington,
D.C., who has written a paper on *The Villain in Wuthering
Heights*. The villain in *Wuthering Heights* is no other than
Ellen Dean, the housekeeper, 'one of the consummate
villains in English literature', as he calls her, 'perhaps the
most obviously neurotic woman' in the Brontë canon,
whose resentment and jealousy and implacable ambition,
not to mention her cruelty, are the mainspring of the
whole action and the cause of the tragedy. This is an
extreme example, if you like, but it is far from being the
only one. We are all familiar with the theories of Emily's
secret love affair, which did so much damage to her
psyche. Once, disastrously for one of her biographers, it
was 'Louis Parensell' who was the lover. (Charlotte's
illegible handwriting, scribbling 'Love's Farewell' on one
of Emily's poems, was responsible for that one.) Once, in
French, it was some dynamic young ploughboy or farm-
hand, encountered in a moorland hollow. And there has
been no lack of suggestion that it was her incestuous love

for Branwell which darkened her imagination, or a
Lesbian attachment to Anne, which turned out badly.
And lately, since anyone who has ever written about the
Brontës is bound to be treated to the theories of other
people, I have encountered in more than one quarter a
new rumour which will lead, I am told, to a sensational
revelation (I shall not be here to hear it) in the year 1999.
A family in Liverpool, the rumour goes, or it may be
Manchester, has letters to prove to an astonished world
that Emily's secret love-affair was with Mr Brontë. There
is a pendant to this, of course. *The Incest Theme in
Wuthering Heights*—the title of another paper, this time
by a Harvard professor—prepared us some twenty years
ago for such a development. 'One need not,' says the
author of it, 'follow the dark Freudian lines of the Emily–
Branwell relationship . . . to prove Emily Brontë's
familiarity with the concept of incestuous connections',
and he goes on to explain the anguish of the Heathcliff–
Catherine relationship by the theory that Catherine and
Heathcliff are brother and sister. 'How?' one may ask,
remembering the story. It is quite simple. Heathcliff is Mr
Earnshaw's illegitimate child, hidden in the Liverpool
slums until the age of seven, and brought home by his
doting father, to the destruction of the family. And if one
asks what support he brings forward for this inspiration it
turns out, disappointingly enough, to be only this—'that
an unconsciously incestuous love between the two leading
characters *would not run counter* to the tone of a novel filled
with violent and savage scenes'.

'Well, is that all?' one is tempted to say. But the idea
has taken root; and now the Rev Patrick Brontë is
involved, and goodness knows where it will end. There is

even a sort of sequel already, which I encountered before
I had recovered from the first shock. 'Why,' said this
further whisper, 'did Emily *really* leave Law Hill, after
only six months or so there as a teacher? She was there
longer than that it seems, or somewhere else. There is a
mysterious gap when she is never mentioned or referred
to. It can have only one meaning!' Yes, yes, I know. And
before long we shall hear that the child was abandoned
somewhere, probably in a snowstorm, à la Gondal. And
so on and so on.

I think it unprofitable to follow such unlikely rumours,
and I mention them only to express my exasperation.
Ellis Bell might well have wondered what was meant, and
have suspected the theorist of more than affectation. Yet
one understands well enough how these theories come into
being. Emily Brontë's small body of work—one novel,
and a collection, not large, of poems of very variable
quality, is so extraordinary, considering her background
and the few known facts of her life, that it is impossible to
stop oneself wondering and trying to explain it. Her reserve and secrecy defeat us at every turn. Every track has
been erased, every earth stopped. Well may we say, as Mrs
Reed's maid said of Jane Eyre, 'I never saw a girl of her
age with so much cover.' Even the monumental work done
on the Gondal saga by Miss Fannie Ratchford, though it
is full of interest and suggestion, opens as many dangerous as illuminating possibilities. We can, after all, take
our choice of at least three theories, and to support it,
whichever it is, there is an equal amount of evidence to be
found in the poems. Indeed, as Miss Ratchford herself has
said, 'Emily's poems afford ample evidence—judiciously
selected—to support *any* theory.'

We can believe, for instance, that most of the poems, and the origins of *Wuthering Heights*, belong to Gondal, to a wholly imaginary world. It is perfectly possible to believe this of Emily, even in her twenties, and I sometimes incline to this view. Or one can equally well suppose—and Derek Stanford has made out an excellent case in his analysis of the poems—that Gondal is a cover, a mask, a disguise, through which Emily speaks with her own voice. This is a very tempting but treacherous theory, chiefly responsible for those learned papers on incest and infanticide motifs, constructions based on sexual symbolism, guilt, and so on. Or we can take the view, which as far as I can see is the most reasonable, that Emily's work must be taken as partly one, partly the other, and that whichever it is—this is important—*we can never know*. Remembering her anger when the poems were first discovered by Charlotte, I cannot help reflecting, in the end, that our total bafflement must be giving her spirit a grim sort of satisfaction. There is even a certain pleasure, a kind of back-handed compliment to Emily, in admitting the impenetrability of the camouflage. She meant to keep her secret, and she has. Our discomfiture is the measure of her success.

Withdrawing gingerly from Gondal, a territory as tricky as a tidal marsh, I would like to return to the somewhat firmer ground of *Wuthering Heights*. (Though that, too, may be an illusion.) It is true that the prevailing atmosphere is one of violence and storm, that most of its characters are 'not nice', and perform savage and violent acts. But perhaps too much dismay has been expressed, both by early reviewers and later critics, that such an atmosphere, and such acts, should have risen in the mind of a Yorkshire parson's daughter. I am not at all trying to minimise the strangeness of the novel; it is, indeed, 'bottomlessly strange'; but I suspect too little thought has been given to the moral climate of the time and the part of the country in which Emily Brontë lived and had her being. Sir Victor Pritchett, I believe, in an article in *The New Statesman* called 'The Implacable, Belligerent People of Wuthering Heights', is the only writer who has dared to say in print that the natives of remote parts of Yorkshire are still very often implacable, full of egotism, resolute in hatred, and often so blunt in speech that 'but for a quizzical glitter in the eyes of the speaker, one might have taken their words as challenge, insult, or derision'. 'I can think of episodes,' he says, 'in my own childhood among them, which are as extraordinary as some of the things in *Wuthering Heights*; and which, at first sight, would strike the reader as examples of pitiable hatred and harshness. Often they were. But really their fierceness in criticism, the pride, and the violence of their sense of sin was the expression of a view of life which put energy and the will of man above everything else. To survive in these parts one had to dominate and oppose.' I do not wish to labour this point further, but would like to suggest that, if these attributes are still observable today, they were even more pronounced a century ago, and that the action of *Wuthering Heights* is set still further back, in the last two decades of the eighteenth century. Farms and human lives were unimaginably remote, by modern standards; self-absorption, private feuds and revenges, had a rich soil to grow in. And the people of unpopulous country districts, even today, are not always as nice in their susceptibilities as some people would have us believe. I am thinking of

two incidents in *Wuthering Heights* which are often
quoted as examples of quite gratuitous cruelty—
Heathcliff's hanging of Isabella Linton's spaniel on the
night when he runs off with her (an act which is plainly
stated as having been done to make her hate him), and
that other incident where Hareton as a child is discovered
in the kitchen, hanging a litter of puppies from the back
of a chair. Have we forgotten that within living memory,
still more so in the eighteenth century, hanging was the
method by which unwanted dogs and puppies were
disposed of? Boswell on the Grand Tour hanged his dog
without a second thought because it failed to keep up
with the carriage, and his reputation is not that of a
brutal man. I well remember, just before the last war, my
own disgust when a neighbouring farmer hanged a sheep-
dog; the animal was sick and he concluded that it had
picked up poison. His cheerful excuse was that the dog
was ill, and he wasn't going to waste shot. And more
recently than that, a young farmer's daughter who worked
for me, an amiable girl, told me one morning that they
had hardly been able to eat their breakfast for laughing,
since Father had hanged the Christmas goose on the
stable door, and the family had laughed themselves sick
at the creature's struggles. Yet another episode comes to
mind from my own childhood, when I read such essays as
Infanticide and Sadism in Wuthering Heights which are so
popular in American literary studies. The harsh treatment
of the children in the story, especially Heathcliff's
deliberate destruction of his son Linton, are held up as
revealing examples of wicked perversity. What is perverse
at one time, and in one culture, may well not be so in
another, and the crime I am thinking of, which happened

further north, in Scotland, was evidently not so regarded by the people who committed it. I used to be sent for the summer holidays, with a cousin of my own age, to a lonely farm belonging to my cousin's grandparents. The farmer's wife, her grandmother, was a kindly woman with a great tenderness for 'the bairns', and when one day a gipsy woman (tinkers, I think they were called) came to the door with an infant in her arms, she bustled about for shawls and things to give her. A few weeks later the tinkers with their cart passed by again, and this time the woman appeared without a baby. My cousin's grandmother asked to see the child, which she supposed was in the cart, but 'Och, no,' said the gipsy's wife, 'it didna thrive, and my man slew it.' There was no attempt at concealment; the thing was stated as reasonable, like the hanging of a puppy; and remembering the degraded conditions in which the boy Heathcliff was found, and the hints of his gipsy origin, his cruelty to the sickly Linton seems to me not diabolical, as it is often described, but the manifestation of a callousness entirely in tune with his nature and probable origin.

What *is* his nature, though? For Heathcliff is one of the Emily Brontë enigmas, about whom there is much disagreement. Catherine Earnshaw, from first to last, has been recognised as a creation unique in literature—wild, headstrong, selfish, high-spirited, maddening in behaviour; even, towards the end of her short life, a little mad (there is that curiously modern-sounding phrase, 'her mental illness')—yet utterly real, utterly convincing, utterly fascinating. Heathcliff has had a much more varied critical career. He shocked Charlotte Brontë, as we know; to her he was 'a ghoul, an afreet'—and indeed, I

saw what she meant when, in Africa, I was under the
influence of fever and the rainy season. Some later critics
see him simply as a survival from the age of the Gothic
novel, a Bridegroom of Barna, a piece of Byronic extravagance, a schoolgirl's chimaera. He has often been compared to Iago for sheer unaccountable wickedness. He has
been dismissed as totally incredible, a pasteboard and
melodrama figure, and one must admit that one or two of
his pronouncements are distinctly 'ham'. He has also been
hailed as a man born before his time, a forerunner of the
modern anti-hero; and there is something in that,
perhaps, in spite of his Gothic ancestry. It is not his
amorality, his harshness, revengefulness or avarice that we
find difficult to swallow today, so much as the lifelong
intensity of his passion. His gnashings and foamings, his
'sharp cannibal teeth', his eyes like 'clouded windows of
hell' from which a 'fiend' looks out, do perhaps help one
to understand what E. M. Forster meant when he spoke
of the necessity of suspending one's sense of humour; but
these are Gothic trimmings left over from an earlier period,
for which Charlotte and Branwell also had a weakness; they
go with those occasional gargoyle phrases—I can think of
only two, Charlotte has many more—'previous to inspect-
ing the penetralium' for 'before going indoors', or 'maxillary
convulsions' to indicate Heathcliff's agonised grimaces.

There is no doubt that Emily, like Charlotte before her,
was strongly drawn to the dark, violent, menacing type of
hero. He pervades Gondal as well as Angria, and neither
Charlotte nor Emily dreams of condemning him because
of his egotism, ruthlessness, or menace. In fact, when
considering Heathcliff, in the absence of the Emperor
Julius's life or any other Gondal chronicle, it is helpful to

look at the heroes of some of Charlotte's Angrian histories. At Percy, Earl of Northangerland, for instance, in the days before Charlotte's Puritan conscience got the upper hand.

Once Emily's imagination, in some ways not dissimilar from Charlotte's, was engaged with the alluringly sinister character who became Heathcliff, her visionary powers, like Charlotte's almost trance-like, brought him to life and clothed him with attributes and qualities long before (I suspect) she began her novel. How strong that visionary power was, *Wuthering Heights* itself bears witness. Emily has left no account of the extraordinary depth of daydream they both indulged in, but Charlotte has; her diary of the Roe Head period, when she was twenty-one, contains passages which suggest that the experience verged on hallucination. Listen to this; it is the onset of the hallucinated mood. Charlotte is in charge of a class, on a winter evening, writing with her eyes shut (a mediumistic touch) while the pupils presumably get on with their prep. and she listens to the night wind. 'That wind, pouring in impetuous current through the air, sounding wildly, unremittingly, from hour to hour, deepening its tone as the night advances, coming not in gusts, but with a rapid, gathering stormy swell—that wind I know is heard at this moment far away on the moors of Haworth. Branwell and Emily hear it, and as it sweeps over our house, down the churchyard and round the old church, they think, perhaps, of me and Anne! Glorious! that blast was mighty; it reminded me of Northangerland . . .' And she is off, eyes closed, pen moving, phantoms rising. And a page or two later, having heard from Branwell that in *his* chronicles Zamorna is in retreat and has evacuated and burned Adrianopolis—'Last night'—it is a windy night again, both sisters are vibrantly responsive to the wind—'Last night I did indeed lean upon the thunder-waking winds of such a stormy blast as I have seldom heard blow, and it whirled me away like heath in the wilderness for five seconds of ecstasy; and as I sat by myself in the dining-room while all the rest were at tea, the trance seemed to descend on a sudden, and verily this foot trod the war-shaken shores of the Calabar, and these eyes saw the defiled and violated Adrianopolis shedding its lights on the river from lattices whence the invader looked out.'

This is a long disgression, perhaps, but it leads me back to Heathcliff, whom Emily conceived, I dare say, by very much the same process, and projected, for all his strangeness, with a clarity and conviction that are almost physical. I am inclined to believe that Emily's visionary life was more intense, more auto-hypnotic and trance-like even than Charlotte's, and that only the purity of her prose, which has no purple passages, was the magic by which fantasy was changed into something real. For Heathcliff *is* real, whatever some may say; he is a mytho-poeic character, he has created his own legend; and I do not even find him diabolical when my temperature is normal. He is an obsessional character, a man with a powerful one-track mind, warped by the brutality of his early experiences and pursuing his revenges with a ruthlessness which is thoroughly and cruelly logical. What Emily Brontë *meant* by him, of course, who is to say? The question of what any novelist *means* by a particular character is invariably a vexed one. The most powerful creations are often not those that are drawn

direct from life, but which rise unbidden and even un-
recognised from the subconscious, an area possible to
guess at, but not explore. 'A novel's true subject,' says an
American critic, one of the more sensible ones, 'is the one
that, regardless of the novelist's *conscious* intention,
actually informs the work, the one that elicits the most
highly energised writing.' Charlotte Brontë said the same
thing rather differently; perhaps better. 'This I know,' she
wrote, in the preface to the second edition of *Wuthering
Heights*: 'the writer who possesses the creative gift owns
something of which he is not always master—something
that at times strangely wills and works for itself.' The
characters which, in Thomas Moser's words, 'elicit the
most highly energised writing' in *Wuthering Heights* are,
of course, without question, Heathcliff and the first
Catherine. Others are splendidly conceived; the younger
Catherine is enchanting, Linton detestable yet pitiable,
Edgar Linton convincing in his negative way, Ellen Dean
the camera's eye, reassuring and omniscient narrator. But
it is Heathcliff and Cathy, those elementals, who are the
ones we remember all our lives; it is their passion that
dictates the theme, maintains the melodic line; and since
their fierce essence surely was distilled from the in-
accessible matrix of the imagination, we can assume that
the germs of both of them were in Emily Brontë, somewhere. But in what form, and how they came there, none
can tell. More than twenty years ago, writing about the
Brontë sisters, I did my best to arrive at at least a tentative
conclusion about these things: about the psychic injury
that Emily suffered, the real or subjective experience of
rejection, the turning inward and the ascent of what Derek
Stanford has called a spiritual ladder with three rungs—

stoicism, pantheism, quietism; and what I said then I have since found no reason to modify. Of the many studies of Emily Brontë which have been written in the last twenty years I have found Derek Stanford's exploration of her poetry the most helpful.* It goes nearer to the heart of the matter than anything else I know of, and has enlarged my appreciation of Emily's poetry, to which I am less receptive, perhaps, than some people. The book I am speaking of is in two parts: in the first and very much shorter section Mrs Muriel Spark examines the biographical material about Emily, whom she sees, not as the centre of a galaxy of sexual symbols, but as a 'born celibate'; and this, too, I find admirable, since I share her impatience with the self-identification of some of Emily's biographers, and respect her refusal to deal with anything that is not evidence. I would not go so far as to agree with her that 'it seems likely that if she (Emily) had not died of consumption, she would have died mentally deranged.' But 'something corrosive', she says, near the end, 'had laid hold of Emily's being', and against this, considering the tenor of her poems, and the disturbing, the almost perverse courage with which she embraced death, I find myself unable to argue.

Let us cheer ourselves by returning to *Wuthering Heights*, for in spite of the tragedy, the sombreness, the strangeness, the final impression made by the novel—and it increases with every reading—is one of profound pleasure. I do not mean only the true catharsis which comes with the death of Heathcliff and the peace and reconciliation of the final chapters: I mean pleasure in the

---

* *Emily Brontë: Her Life and Work.* Muriel Spark and Derek Stanford (1953).

sense of delight and illumination, of a thousand small
surprises and revelations which are the gifts of that seeing
eye, that wonderful prose. One could make an anthology
simply out of those passages in which Emily observes and
invokes the moorland weather. It is not done with purple
passages or great set pieces; each word is simple, and falls
quietly into place. One is reminded of that observation of
Charlotte's which Mrs Gaskell found so moving: that it
was remarkable what a companion the sky was, to a
solitary person. The sky, the wind, the heath, the mist
lying in Gimmerton valley, the raving of the brooks after a
night of rain, the whirling suffocation of the snow, the
calm effulgence of moonlight on a winter landscape—all
these were more than a companion to] Emily Brontë.
Without falsifying, her spirit identified with them.
Indeed, as Lord David Cecil has said in his memorable
essay: 'No other writer gives us such a feeling of naked
contact with actual earth and water ... To read Emily
Brontë's descriptions after those of most authors, is like
leaving an exhibition of landscape paintings to step into
the open air.'

In these descriptions, simple and unadorned as they
are, it is the poet speaking. She has performed, perhaps
unconsciously, that extremely difficult technical feat of
transmuting poetry into prose. It is a question of rhythm
and ear, and Emily was not only a poet, she was the
musical one of the family. Listen to the alliteration in the
latter part of this long sentence, in which the younger
Catherine is describing her delight in 'rocking in a
rustling green tree, with a west wind blowing ...' and
'close by great swells of long grass undulating in waves to
the breeze, and woods and sounding water, and the whole

world awake and wild with joy.' One lingers with delight over innumerable passages, and many of the speeches of Heathcliff and Catherine, though nakedly simple in diction, have the rhythm and the ring of irregular verse. Consider these lines, which have an almost Whitmanesque proportion: 'What is not connected with her to me? and what does not recall her? I cannot look down to this floor, but her features are shaped in the flags! In every cloud, in every tree—filling the air at night and caught by glimpses in every object by day—I am surrounded with her image! The most ordinary faces of men and women—my own features—mock me with a resemblance. The entire world is a dreadful collection of memoranda that she did exist, and that I have lost her!'

And here is another delight, smaller and less poetical, but exactly right; having the quality of a rather touching surprise, since perhaps the last thing one expects to find at Wuthering Heights is a toy cupboard. It is the younger Catherine speaking: 'After sitting still an hour, I looked at the great room with its smooth uncarpeted floor, and thought how nice it would be to play in, if we removed the table; and I asked Linton to call Zillah in to help us, and we'd have a game of blind man's buff; she should try to catch us; you used to, you know, Ellen. He wouldn't: there was no pleasure in it, he said; but he consented to play at ball with me. We found two in a cupboard, among a heap of old toys, tops, and hoops, and battledores, and shuttlecocks. One was marked C., and the other H.; I wished to have the C., because that stood for Catherine, and the H. might be for Heathcliff, his name; but the bran came out of H., and Linton didn't like it.' Not only a delightful childish scene, but a startling reminder that even Heathcliff had bowled a hoop in his lighter moments, and joined Catherine in a fast game of battledore and shuttlecock.

There are so many small pleasures of this or another kind, little details deliberately dropped that send one off on interesting speculations, that I am tempted to mention one or two more. The great importance, for instance, that books play in *Wuthering Heights*, as they did in the life of Emily Brontë and of all at Haworth Parsonage. L. P. Hartley in a letter once asked me if I had observed Emily Brontë's great respect for education, as evinced in the novel. It had not struck me in quite those terms, but the books I *had* noticed. Emily, more than any other writer, perhaps, found 'tongues in trees, books in the running brooks, sermons in stones'; but books themselves were a great source of light and comfort. 'A few mildewed books piled up in one corner' are the only relics of Catherine Earnshaw that Lockwood finds on the window-sill at the beginning of the story. She has written a great deal— presumably in a hand as cramped as Emily's—on the spare leaves of one of them, being short of writing paper. We know that she was a great reader, and so was her daugher Catherine, who learned a great deal of poetry by heart, and could recite many ballads. The severest punishment which Heathcliff inflicts on her at Wuthering Heights is to destroy her books. Heathcliff, we are told, never reads; and one feels this is a black mark against him. It is books that Catherine uses to bribe the groom to saddle the pony for secret excursions to the Heights. Edgar Linton practically lives in his library; it is there that he takes refuge in perplexity and grief, there that he educates his daughter. Even Ellen (to account for her fluency, no doubt) has made good use of it. 'You could not open a book in this library', she tells Mr Lockwood, 'that I have not looked into, and got something out of also.' And Lockwood himself, after some months at the Grange, exclaims, 'Take my books away, and I should be desperate!' Hareton, the illiterate oaf, becomes even more dependent on them; his purloining the younger Catherine's books, though he can scarcely read, is the beginning of their love-affair and reconciliation. All this shows that L. P. Hartley was right as usual; education, to Emily Brontë, is a magic talisman. Hareton is redeemed by it, and made not only presentable but lovable. And Mr Shielders, now—does anyone remember him? He was the curate, who educated not only the young Lintons, but also Hindley and Catherine Earnshaw and, in the early days, Heathcliff. And Heathcliff himself, though he no longer reads, seems to consider education important, since he pays a tutor to come three times a week for Linton, and from twenty miles away. A hundred and twenty miles of riding each week, as well as the hours of teaching! Heathcliff, we know, was mean, and it must have been expensive.

When I find, as I do here, that I have scribbled a few further notes to consider, they are usually on small points in *Wuthering Heights* which have caused me to wonder a little. There are a good many deaths, for instance, in the novel, and at first sight—although of course they are essential to the development of the plot—they seem to come about in that unexplained, early Victorian way which a hundred years and more ago was accepted without question. (One has only to think of Mrs Gaskell's innumerable death-beds.) But a closer attention shows us that most of them have a probability that was only too familiar in the 1840s, and of which there had been, and were to be again, tragic examples at home in Haworth Parsonage. We are not told what Mr Earnshaw died of; age and disease are mentioned; he dies quietly in his chair. Remembering that a few years before he had walked to Liverpool and back, a distance of 120 miles, in three days, and for the return sixty miles had carried a seven-year-old child, one wonders if his heart had been permanently damaged. The first Catherine goes through several illnesses; she and Heathcliff have measles as children, and at fifteen she 'catches a fever', which is not specified, apart from our being told that it was dangerous, and that she was delirious. What that fever was I am not sure; Emily would have known about the great cholera epidemic in Manchester in the 1830s, and there were outbreaks of typhus, one remembers, at Cowan Bridge. At all events, it was a highly contagious infection, for when Mrs Linton took Catherine to Thrushcross Grange for convalescence, she and her husband 'both took the fever, and died within a few days of each other.' Later, when Catherine is married to Edgar Linton and already pregnant, after a scene of great violence and hysteria, she shuts herself up on hunger strike until she becomes ill with brain fever. It is spoken of by Nelly Dean as a 'mental illness', and it is made clear that though she does not die of it, there is some deep psychic damage; she is permanently changed, and it is against a background of mental unbalance and deep trauma that the last, most agonising scene between the lovers takes place. Catherine dies, not specifically of her illness, but in childbirth, when the second Catherine is born later that night. Six months afterwards her brother Hindley dies of drink—a misfortune not unknown in Haworth village, and soon to be witnessed at first hand in the Parsonage, a year after *Wuthering Heights* was published. The second and third generations of Lintons—here again there is an uncanny feeling of prophecy—all die of tuberculosis: Edgar, his sister Isabella, and her son Linton. The symptoms of Linton's peevish and pitiable decline, softened by neither nursing nor kindness, apart from Catherine's nightmare death-watch, is one of the most harrowingly realistic accounts in fiction. It is perhaps not surprising, considering the period and the then primitive state of medical knowledge, that Emily Brontë should have been so concerned with illness and death. She dwells on it, not from excessive morbidity, or solely for the plot, but because it was a part of daily life in the 'forties, which she had known, and was soon to know again, at first hand.

Heathcliff's death, after all, is the only real mystery, the only one that points straight into that dark but exalted region where it is so difficult to follow her. It is often said that he deliberately starves himself to death, in his passionate yearning to be reunited with the dead Catherine, and certainly his triumphant death-wish plays a part in it. But self-starvation is not the answer; he fasts, in all, for only four days and nights, and that, to a man of his 'hard constitution and temperate mode of living' would have been nothing. Nelly, we remember, mentions his 'strange illness'; and if it is possible for a man to die by an effort of will, by an overwhelming conviction of the spirit, as Africans have been known to die when the finger has pointed at them, then I believe that this is how we are meant to take it. It is the reverse of the African's acceptance; it is a triumph, a feat of the spirit, and I am sure there is no irony in that wonderful, that too often quoted closing paragraph, in which the storms and discordant elements are resolved at last, and the peace of non-being obliterates the pains of death.

The division between life and death, for Emily Brontë, was at times a tenuous and transparent one. The whole unspoken theme of *Wuthering Heights* is somehow to do with this, and if we could clearly grasp it we would have the key to her mystery. Her ecstatic response to the natural world, her awareness of that other, unseen yet all-pervading, the power of her prose and the cryptic utterances of her verses, would cohere into a great design, and we should ask no more questions. One cannot formulate it in words, but the conviction remains: under the music of everything that Emily Brontë wrote the echo of Heathcliff's leap into the dark reverberates again and again like a roll of drums.

4
Charlotte Brontë and Elizabeth Gaskell – the Fruitful Friendship

4

Charlotte Brontë and Elizabeth Gaskell — the Fruitful Friendship

WHEN I LOOK at the long bookshelf on which I keep everything I possess to do with the Brontës and Mrs Gaskell, I cannot help thinking how much poorer we would be, and also how much Mrs Gaskell and Charlotte Brontë would have missed, if those two remarkable women had never met.

It was not, after all, a long friendship—only 4 years and 7 months between their first meeting in a house on Lake Windermere in August 1850 and Charlotte's death in Haworth on the last day of March, 1855. Each gave to the other something precious and rare, which probably no-one else in the world had the power to give. Charlotte's gift to Mrs Gaskell was in a sense a reciprocal one, of equal importance to them both. Without knowing it, or even dreaming of such a thing, she gave Mrs Gaskell the subject and inspiration of perhaps her greatest work, a literary masterpiece. And Mrs Gaskell, in return, again unconsciously or almost so, was preparing to give to posterity a portrait, an interpretation of Charlotte Brontë, both as woman and writer, which has added incalculably both to Charlotte's own fame, and to our own knowledge and appreciation.

Imagine how different the whole Brontë scene would be

if Mrs Gaskell had not recognised, and accepted, the task that lay before her; if those whom Mr Brontë contemptuously described as 'a great many scribblers' had been the only contemporaries to write about her life! Already, as we know, a fortnight *before* Mr Brontë's urgent request reached her, Mrs Gaskell had felt impelled to record all that she had learned from, and about, Charlotte during their four years' intimacy. 'I cannot tell you', she wrote to George Smith, 'how I honoured and loved her . . . Some time, it may be years hence—but if I live long enough, and no-one is living whom such a publication would hurt, I will publish what I know of her, and make the world (if I am but strong enough in expression) honour the woman as much as they admired the writer.'

Anyone who has ever undertaken a biography knows what a vital, what a precious, element a *personal* intimacy between writer and subject can be. It has, in one sense, its disadvantages, when personal loyalties and discretions intervene, and things are suppressed which a less sensitive posterity wants to know about. But that personal knowledge, affection, understanding, are invaluable. Where would we be without Boswell's *Johnson*, Forster's *Dickens*, and indeed, Mrs Gaskell's *Charlotte Brontë*? These are the great foundations on which later biographers for ever and ever build. Some of these, of course, have sharply criticised Mrs Gaskell's work, feeling that they—naturally—could have done it so much better. Of course she made a few mistakes, and of course was guilty of a few delicate suppressions; but I am still convinced that Charlotte Brontë's fame and literary status would not be quite what it is today if she had not formed that fruitful friendship with Elizabeth Gaskell.

The Fruitful Friendship

So there we see it as a reciprocal gift—two friends conferring an imperishable fame on one another. And it was not only in the sphere of literature that they mutually benefited: a personal sympathy developed rapidly at that first meeting, and had an unforeseen effect on Charlotte's life, as we shall see later. What would we do without Mrs Gaskell's letters—so rapid, so long, so lively—dashing off to her friends the great news of having actually met Currer Bell, the author of that slightly shocking best-seller, *Jane Eyre*, who was really Miss Brontë, a curate's daughter, and what an altogether surprising little person she found her!

It is a Sunday evening, at Briery Close near Windermere, and after being driven from the station by the Kay-Shuttleworths' coachman, Mrs Gaskell is shown into 'a pretty drawing-room . . . in which were Sir James and Lady K.S., and a little lady in a black silk gown, whom I couldn't see at first for the dazzle in the room. She came up and shook hands with me at once. I went up to un-bonnet etc., came down to tea; the little lady worked away'—at needlework, of course—'and hardly spoke; but I had time for a good look at her. She is (as she calls herself) *undeveloped*; thin and more than half a head shorter than I, soft brown hair not so dark as mine; eyes (very good and expressive looking straight and open at you) of the same colour; a reddish face; a large mouth and many teeth gone; altogether *plain;* the forehead square, broad, and rather overhanging. She has a very sweet voice, rather hesitates in choosing her expressions, but when chosen they seem . . . *admirable* and *just* befitting the occasion. There is nothing overstrained but perfectly simple.' 'Poor thing,' Mrs Gaskell wrote to her friend

85

Tottie Fox, 'she can hardly smile, she has led such a hard, cruel (if one may dare to say so) life . . . The wonder to me is how she can have kept heart and power alive in her life of desolation.'

What a different impression Mrs Gaskell must have made on Charlotte Brontë! She, at not quite forty, was still beautiful: she possessed that indefinable quality known as 'charm': her manner was easy and attractive: she was thoroughly used to an exhaustingly crowded social life and had never been shy. Her home background was as different from Charlotte's as one can possibly imagine, always frantically busy, with a highly intelligent and likeable husband and a house full of little girls, as well as her own work and all the duties and responsibilities that burdened a conscientious minister's wife in Manchester.

Charlotte's life, as we know, had already entered that unspeakably lonely and melancholy phase, when she was so solitary and depressed that she found it difficult to communicate with anyone. Branwell, Emily and Anne were all dead. Her own health was often wretched, and with Mr Brontë immured in his silent parlour the house was as quiet as a tomb. Charlotte's unhappy love for M. Heger had been a slowly diminishing anguish for almost six years, and was not yet, I suspect, entirely overcome. There is an ominous sentence in *Jane Eyre*, like an uneasy prophecy—'It is madness in all women to let a secret love kindle within them, which, if unreturned and unkown, must devour the life that feeds it.' And another disturbing and stoical passage which seems to express both Charlotte's deep unhappiness, and also her strength: 'I rose. I looked back at the bed I had left. Hopeless of the future, I wished but this—that my Maker had that night thought good to require my soul of me while I slept; and that this weary frame, absolved by death from further conflict with fate, had now but to decay quietly, and mingle in peace with the soil of this wilderness. Life, however, was yet in my possession: with all its require- ments, and pains, and responsibilities. The burden must be carried; the want provided for; the suffering endured; the responsibility fulfilled. I set out.'

This, then, was the silent, stoical and unhappy atmo- sphere of Charlotte's life at the time when Mrs Gaskell entered it, and brought into it a ray of warmth and light. Charlotte found it possible, not only to communicate, but even to confide in her new friend. 'I could never rest'— again it is Jane Eyre speaking—'I could never rest in communication with strong, discreet and refined minds, whether male or female, till I had passed the outworks of conventional reserve, and crossed the threshold of confidence, and won a place by their heart's very hearth- stone.' Later, both at Plymouth Grove and in the Parson- age at Haworth, it was at this very hearthstone that the two of them spent long hours of intimate talk, and it seems that in Mrs Gaskell Charlotte found a confidante far more seductive—if that is the right word, perhaps I should say 'receptive'—than either of her old friends Ellen Nussey or Mary Taylor. Ellen, good, kind, affectionate creature that she was, had little intellectual or imaginative perception, and so had never been allowed into the labyrinths of Charlotte's imaginative life. And Mary Taylor, more intelligent and experienced in many ways than Ellen, had disappeared to Australia five years ago, and was out of reach except for occasional letters. It was Mrs Gaskell's rare qualities of sympathy and charm that opened the doors of communication, so that, sitting together by the fire long after Mr Brontë had gone to bed, she heard some strange stories of Charlotte's childhood with her brother and sisters, of her sister Maria's death and of 'those strange starved days at school', of her experiences as a governess, and of the two periods in Brussels—all of it directly communicated in long reminiscent conversations, with none of the exaggerations and inaccuracies of Lady Kay-Shuttleworth's breathless gossip to Mrs Gaskell several years before. 'We were so happy together,' Mrs Gaskell wrote later, 'we were so full of interest in each other's subjects. The day seemed only too short for what we had to say and to hear.' And when the day was drawing to a close, 'We have generally had another walk before tea, which is at six; at half-past eight, prayers; and by nine, all the household are in bed, except ourselves. We sit up together till ten, or past; and after I go, I hear Miss Brontë come down and walk up and down the room for an hour or so.' That restless pacing up and down in the midnight hours no doubt told Mrs Gaskell as much as any of the confidences—'that slow, monotonous, incessant walk,' she wrote, 'in which I am sure *I* should fancy I heard the steps of the dead following me. She says she could not sleep without it—that she and her sisters talked over the plans and projects of their whole lives at such times.'

On their walks over the moors, then, and in these late-night sessions, Mrs Gaskell asked many questions from her own knowledge as a writer, especially about the description of happenings outside Charlotte's own experience. For such imaginings, Charlotte told her, she

'thought intently for many and many a night before falling
to sleep — wondering what it was like, or how it would be
— till at length, sometimes after the progress of her story
had been arrested at this one point for weeks, she wakened
up in the morning with all clear before her, as if she had in
reality gone through the experience, and then could
describe it, word for word, as it had happened. I cannot
account for this psychologically,' Mrs Gaskell owned; 'I
am only sure that it was so because she said it.' This
technique of the imagination, often as vivid in impression
as an opium dream, was something that Charlotte
had practised from her earliest years, from the days of the
Angrian romances. In times of unhappiness or stress, it
had been, as she said, her 'sole relief' to 'pace backwards
and forwards, safe in the silence and solitude of the spot,
and allow my mind's eye to dwell on whatever bright
visions rose before it ... and best of all, to open my
inward ear to a tale that was never ended—a tale my
imagination created, and narrated continuously; quick-
ened with all of incident, life, fire, feeling, that I desired,
and had not in my actual experience.' Those, of course,
are the words of Jane Eyre, but they could equally well
have been a passage in Charlotte's own diary. So, indeed,
are the passionate words that follow:

'Women are supposed to be very calm generally; but
women feel, just as men feel; they need exercise for their
faculties, and a field for their efforts as much as their
brothers do; they suffer from too rigid a constraint, too
absolute a stagnation, precisely as men would suffer; and
it is narrow-minded ... to say that they ought to confine
themselves to making puddings and knitting stockings, to
playing on the piano and embroidering bags.' What a

surprisingly modern, not to say psycho-analytical point of
view! It was this depth and passion in Charlotte which so
astonished and impressed Mrs Gaskell, so that even at the
time the idea began to suggest itself that one day she
must write down all that she remembered of Miss Brontë,
so that nothing of this memorable experience should be
lost. And Charlotte's response to Mrs Gaskell was
equally intense. 'After you left,' she wrote, 'the house felt
very much as if the shutters had been suddenly closed and
the blinds let down. One was sensible during the re-
mainder of the day of a depressing silence, shadow, loss,
and want.'

'I was aware,' Mrs Gaskell wrote later, 'that she had a
great anxiety on her mind at this time; and being ac-
quainted with its nature, I could not but deeply admire
the patient docility which she displayed in her conduct
towards her father.' So, a part of those late-night conversations, as we learn from that discreet statement, had been
to do with the unlucky Mr Nicholls, and it is at this point
that we begin to see another, and very important, fruit
beginning to develop out of their fortunate friendship.
Though one cannot prove it, I have always had a strong
feeling that it was largely Mrs Gaskell's influence that
persuaded Charlotte, in spite of lack of love on her part,
and her father's outrageous hostility, that she might do
worse than marry the Irish curate. On a visit to Plymouth
Grove she had told Mrs Gaskell the whole astonishing
story, as far as it had gone, and apparently without any
thought that it could go further. It was only in the
previous December that Mr Nicholls had exploded his
bombshell. 'On Monday evening,' Charlotte had written
at the time to Ellen Nussey, 'Mr Nicholls was here to

tea. I vaguely felt, without clearly seeing, as without seeing I have felt for some time, the meaning of his constant looks, and strange, feverish restraint. After tea I withdrew to the dining-room as usual. As usual, Mr Nicholls sat with Papa till between eight and nine o'clock; I then heard him open the parlour door as if going. I expected the clash of the front door. He stopped in the passage: he tapped: like lightning it flashed upon me what was coming. He entered — he stood before me . . . Shaking from head to foot, looking deadly pale, speaking low, vehemently but with difficulty — he made me for the first time feel what it costs a man to declare affection where he doubts response.'

The infamous behaviour of Mr Brontë on the occasion must have been hard to put up with, and Mrs Gaskell's admiration of Charlotte's self-control was well deserved. 'If I had *loved* Mr Nicholls,' Charlotte wrote, 'and had heard such epithets applied to him as were used, it would have transported me past patience; as it was, my blood boiled with a sense of injustice, but papa worked himself into a state not to be trifled with, the veins on his temples started up like whipcord, and his eyes became suddenly bloodshot.' Mr Brontë, one would guess, was on the verge of a stroke.

So all this was very much in ferment when Mrs Gaskell spent four days with Charlotte at Haworth in September 1853. The battle between Mr Nicholls and Mr Brontë had reached its climax; Mr Nicholls had resigned his curacy and left Haworth. There was no-one to disturb the late-night conversations, and the question of marrying, or *not* marrying if one were not in love, was evidently discussed at length, and without inhibition. Mrs Gaskell,

I feel sure, would have been in favour of the marriage, on the whole, for though Mr Nicholls was no Galahad, still less a Paul Emanuel or Mr Rochester, he was a serious, upright, conscientious man, as passionately in love as any man could be, and this aspect, as Mrs Gaskell guessed, was of great psychological importance. Passionate love was what Charlotte's temperament demanded, and Mrs Gaskell was experienced enough to know that it might, in the end, evoke a happy response. It was certainly not beauty or seductive charm which had ensnared Mr Nicholls; he was aware, in his strange unpromising way, of qualities in her that he believed himself unable to live without; and this, Mrs Gaskell judged, was of great importance. She had herself, when they first met, described the plainness of Charlotte's appearance—that 'ugliness', as Charlotte called it, which caused her so much distress—but she was far too perceptive to have seen it as Thackeray mockingly did, as something which made it impossible for anyone to care for her. (The charming Richmond portrait, of course, is a romantic flattery.) 'The poor little woman of genius!' Thackeray wrote, only a few months before, after reading *Villette*, 'I can read a great deal of her life . . . in her book, and see that rather than have fame, rather than any other earthly good or mayhap heavenly one, she wants some Tomkins or another to love her and be in love with. But you see she is a little bit of a creature without a pennyworth of good looks, thirty years old I should think'—actually she was thirty-six—'buried in the country, and eating up her own heart there, and no Tomkins will come'. But Thackeray was wrong, and Mrs Gaskell was wise enough to see that this particular Tomkins's devotion was much too good to be cast off lightly. 'He sounds vehemently in love with her,' she wrote to John Forster, choosing exactly the right word, 'and I like his having known her dead sisters and dead brother and all she has gone through of home trials, and being no person who has just fancied himself in love with her, because he was dazzled by her genius. ... With all his bigotry and sternness it must be charming to be loved with all the strength of his heart, as she sounds to be ... I am sure Miss Brontë could never have borne not to be well ruled and ordered ... I mean, that she would never have been happy but with an exacting, rigid, law-giving, passionate man.'

Astute Mrs Gaskell! I suspect it may well have been she who, during this period of Mr Nicholls's banishment, persuaded Charlotte that it would not, after all, be so very sinful if she secretly replied to one of poor Mr Nicholls's agonised letters and gave him a hint of encouragement, in spite of her father's inexorable prohibition. This, as we know, Charlotte did, and eventually even met Mr Nicholls in secret, so giving him a chance at last to press his suit, somewhere beyond the sharp gaze of Mr Brontë.

What we *know* that Mrs Gaskell did to forward the affair was to try to remove Mr Brontë's most basic objection to the marriage, which she had learned from Charlotte was financial. *Of course* he would have preferred his daughter to marry someone grand and eminent, who would confer additional fame on the name of Brontë, and of course, having been one himself, there was nothing he despised so much as an obscure Irish curate. (He was not in those days aware of how much better Mr Nicholls's connections were than his own.) But the real basis of the violent objection, as Charlotte freely confessed to Mrs

Gaskell, was the question of money. Mr Nicholls had none of his own, and his salary had had to be paid out of Mr Brontë's own stipend of £250 a year.

This, Mrs Gaskell thought, perhaps lying awake in the spare bedroom at Haworth after one of those late-night sessions, might, with a bit of luck, be rectified. Suppose Charlotte, as an eminent writer, could be awarded a Civil List pension, or something like that? Mrs Gaskell was on friendly terms with Richard Monckton Milnes, the M.P. and philanthropist who was always eager to use his influence with the Royal Literary Fund to help any author in distress, and it occurred to her that a private appeal to him might do the trick. But it would be necessary to discuss it with Charlotte first, and when, tentatively, she broached the subject, it seems that Charlotte shied away from the whole idea, perhaps shrinking from the inevitable publicity. So then, Mrs Gaskell thought, what about a pension or preferment for Mr Nicholls, if only one could think of a good excuse? She discussed the matter with Monckton Milnes, and without giving the game away, got Mr Nicholls's present address from the Haworth postmaster. 'I felt sure you would keep the story secret,' she wrote to Milnes. 'If my well-meant treachery becomes known to her I shall lose her friendship, which I prize most highly.' And then she goes on, 'I have been thinking over little bits of the conversation we had relating to a pension. I do not think she would take it; and I am quite sure that *one* hundred a year given as acknowledgment of his merits, as a good faithful clergyman, would give her *ten* times the pleasure that *two* hundred a year would do, if bestowed upon her in her capacity as a writer. I am sure he is a thoroughly good, hard-working, self-denying curate ... Her father's only reason for his violent and virulent opposition is Mr Nicholls's utter want of money, or friends to help him to any professional advancement.'

Milnes therefore obligingly wrote to Mr Nicholls, much to the latter's surprise, and arranged an interview. It does not appear that anything came of it in the way of a pension or preferment, but Mr Nicholls was encouraged by the contact, so that Mrs Gaskell's efforts were not in vain. 'I can't help fancying,' she wrote to Milnes, 'your kind words may have made him feel he is not so friendless as he represented and believed himself to be at first; and might rouse his despondency up to a fresh effort,' which, as we know, they did. Later, Charlotte gave Mrs Gaskell an unsuspecting account of the interview between Monckton Milnes and Mr Nicholls, and, wrote Mrs Gaskell, 'of the latter's puzzle to account for Mr Milnes' interest in him. He never for an instant suspected anything; or my head would not have been safe on my shoulders.'

Only a few months later Charlotte, her father and Mr Nicholls solved the problem in their own way, since Mr Brontë had become even more exasperated with his new replacement curate than he had ever been with Mr Nicholls, and began to think that even as a son-in-law, and living in the same house, he would be glad to have the Irishman back. And Charlotte, brooding on Mrs Gaskell's sympathetic advice, and looking soberly into the future, had reached the decision that was to turn out so surprisingly well. Of course Mrs Gaskell was aware, from what Charlotte had told her, of the probable disadvantages of Mr Nicholls as a husband. He was not intellectual, and would therefore be unlikely to share in Charlotte's dominant interests. There was a sense, as Charlotte put it, 'of incongruity and uncongeniality of feelings, tastes, principles'. He was a serious High Churchman of the most rigid sort—'a Puseyite and very stiff', Charlotte had told her; 'I fear it will stand in the way of my intercourse with some of my friends'— especially, she obviously meant, the Gaskells, who as Unitarians were, of course, Dissenters. So Mrs Gaskell was aware of the risk that the marriage might turn out badly—a far greater risk in those days than now, for in the 1850's, if things went wrong, one didn't just walk out of the house and get a divorce through the post. Unhappy marriages had to be endured till death, especially if one were a parson's daughter, marrying Father's curate.

But the alternative, as Mrs Gaskell saw it, was far more bleak. Silence and solitude until Mr Brontë died, and after that, silence and solitude somewhere else, made more painful by poverty. At her father's death, Charlotte told Mrs Gaskell, she would inherit £300, apart from what she called 'the little I have earned myself'. If she were ever to marry, she now admitted, it would have to be Mr Nicholls, though she had not yet made up her mind to take the step. Mrs Gaskell, by now almost as deeply involved as Charlotte, gave the latest instalment to Forster, as she had had it from Charlotte herself. 'She said, "Father, I am not a young girl, not a young woman, even—I never was pretty. I now am ugly... Do you think there are many men who would serve seven years for me?" And again when he... asked her if she would marry a curate?—"Yes, I must marry a curate if I marry at all; not merely a curate but *your* curate; not merely *your* curate but he must live in the house with you, for I cannot leave you." The sightless old man stood up and said solemnly, "Never. I will never have another man in this house," and stalked out of the room. For a week he never spoke to her. She had not then made up her mind to accept Mr Nicholls and the worry on both sides made her ill—then the old servant interfered, and asked him, sitting blind and alone, "if he wished to kill his daughter?" . . . and so it has ended where it has done.'

For Charlotte had at last been persuaded to take the risk, and now was 'what people call engaged'. Within a month she was once again visiting Mrs Gaskell, receiving all the encouragement and support she needed, and we have a full and sensitive account of the affair in a letter from Mrs Gaskell's friend Catherine Winkworth, who was with the Gaskells in Manchester at the same time. 'What I hear from Lily', she wrote—'Lily' being short for 'Elizabeth'—'What I hear from Lily of Mr Nicholls is all good.' She tells the story, as she had heard it, up to the previous Christmas. 'Miss Brontë had not then made up her mind; but when she saw him again, she decided that she could make him happy, and that his love is too good to be thrown away by one so lonely as she is; and so they are to be married. He thinks her intellectually superior to himself, and admires her gifts, and likes her the better, which sounds as though he were generous. And has very good family connections . . . and all the parishioners adore him . . . If only he is not altogether too narrow for her, one can fancy her much more really happy with such a man than with one who might have made her more in love . . . But I *guess* the true love was Paul Emmanuel after all, and is dead; but I don't know, and don't think that Lily knows.' But Lily, or rather Elizabeth, was proved right in her instinctive feeling that there was more to Mr Nicholls than appeared on the surface, and that Charlotte might be well advised not to throw him away. What pleasure it must have given her, in the difficult and often agonising task of writing Charlotte's life, when she came to deal with those brief nine months of marriage, when the sombre Mr Nicholls is transformed into 'my dear Arthur', 'my dear Boy', and Charlotte's life, so cruelly cut short, had an aura of happiness at the end.

'I can only say,' Mr Nicholls wrote many years later, 'that during the few months of our married life we were never separated for a day and that during that time a hasty or unkind word never passed between us.'

Which brings me to a final and, to me, very touching glimpse of Mr Nicholls, which I wish Mrs Gaskell could have shared. She had found him inexpressibly difficult during the writing of the biography; the misery and shock of his loss, his intensely private feelings about his marriage she certainly understood, but the understanding did not remove the difficulty. That, and the rows that blew up over Cowan Bridge and other matters upset her so much that she was 'frightened off her nest' as she put it, in a literary sense, for the next six years. I wish she could have realised, though I fear she did not, that the splendid fruit that had come into being from her friendship with Charlotte Brontë was that very biography which gave Charlotte to the world as no-one else could have done. I wish she could have known what Clement Shorter wrote in 1908, when he published *The Brontës: Lives and Letters*. 'It is quite certain,' he wrote in the

Preface, 'that Charlotte Brontë would not stand on so splendid a pedestal today but for the single-minded devotion of her accomplished biographer.'

I wish she could have known something of Mr Nicholls in his later years, for that would have convinced her that, had Charlotte lived and borne her child, her married life would almost certainly have been happy. Several years ago I had the good fortune to meet Mrs Helen Dillon, an old lady who as a child and young girl had been devoted to Mr Nicholls in his old age. After Charlotte's death he had returned to Ireland, nine years later marrying his cousin Mary, who had long been in love with him. He now had no clerical office, but lived a quiet country life as a small gentleman-farmer at Banagher, where Mrs Dillon's father was vicar. She told me much of his love of children and animals, of his playful gentleness with the young people who knew him, not as the 'stern and bigoted' Mr Nicholls but as 'dear Baboo Nick,' the old man who went for walks with them and was fond of lump sugar. Most surprising of all, perhaps, was his long kindness towards Martha Brown, the Haworth Parsonage servant who had once quite 'hated' him, but saw him in a different light after Charlotte's marriage, and to the end of her days made regular and lengthy visits to the Nichollses at Banagher, where she was long remembered for her delicious spongecakes. They corresponded over many years, and in one of Mr Nicholls's surviving letters to her there is a deeply touching reference to Charlotte. Martha had asked for a memento of her late mistress, and remembering those tiny books of stories that Charlotte had written as a child, said that what she would really like was one of these. 'Dear Martha,' Mr

Nicholls wrote, 'I am really very sorry that I can't comply with your request to send you one of the small magazines . . . I got one to enclose to you, but when I looked at the handwriting I could not bring myself to part with it.'

I wish Mrs Gaskell could have known that. And also the recollection—possibly apocryphal—of the nurse who cared for him on his death-bed, that the last words he was ever heard to utter were a whispered repetition—'Charlotte . . . Charlotte . . .'